OPPOSING
VIEWPOINTS®
SERIES

| Virtual Reality

Other Books of Related Interest

Opposing Viewpoints Series

Cybercrime
Robotic Technology
Space Exploration
Video Games

At Issue Series

Does the Internet Increase Crime?
The Wireless Society
What Is the Role of Technology in Education?

Current Controversies Series

Homeschooling
Internet Activism
Mobile Apps

"Congress shall make no law … abridging the freedom of speech, or of the press."

First Amendment to the US Constitution

The basic foundation of our democracy is the First Amendment guarantee of freedom of expression. The Opposing Viewpoints series is dedicated to the concept of this basic freedom and the idea that it is more important to practice it than to enshrine it.

**OPPOSING
VIEWPOINTS®
SERIES**

| Virtual Reality

Susan Henneberg, Book Editor

GREENHAVEN
PUBLISHING

Published in 2017 by Greenhaven Publishing, LLC
353 3rd Avenue, Suite 255, New York, NY 10010

Articles in Greenhaven Publishing anthologies are often edited for length to meet page
requirements. In addition, original titles of these works are changed to clearly present
the main thesis and to explicitly indicate the author's opinion. Every effort is made to
ensure that Greenhaven Publishing accurately reflects the original intent of the authors.
Every effort has been made to trace the owners of the copyrighted material.

Cover image: Yuganov Konstantin/Shutterstock.com

Library of Congress CataloginginPublication Data

Names: Henneberg, Susan.
Title: Virtual reality / Susan Henneberg.
Description: New York : Greenhaven Publishing, 2017. |
Series: Opposing viewpoints | Includes index.
Identifiers: LCCN ISBN 9781534500303 (pbk.) | ISBN 9781534500266 (library bound)
Subjects: LCSH: Virtual reality—Juvenile literature. | Shared virtual environments—
Juvenile literature. | Three-dimensional display systems—Juvenile literature.
Classification: LCC QA76.9.V5 H46 2017 | DDC 006.8—dc23

Manufactured in the United States of America

Website: http://greenhavenpublishing.com

Contents

The Importance of Opposing Viewpoints

Perhaps every generation experiences a period in time in which the populace seems especially polarized, starkly divided on the important issues of the day and gravitating toward the far ends of the political spectrum and away from a consensus-facilitating middle ground. The world that today's students are growing up in and that they will soon enter into as active and engaged citizens is deeply fragmented in just this way. Issues relating to terrorism, immigration, women's rights, minority rights, race relations, health care, taxation, wealth and poverty, the environment, policing, military intervention, the proper role of government—in some ways, perennial issues that are freshly and uniquely urgent and vital with each new generation—are currently roiling the world.

If we are to foster a knowledgeable, responsible, active, and engaged citizenry among today's youth, we must provide them with the intellectual, interpretive, and critical-thinking tools and experience necessary to make sense of the world around them and of the all-important debates and arguments that inform it. After all, the outcome of these debates will in large measure determine the future course, prospects, and outcomes of the world and its peoples, particularly its youth. If they are to become successful members of society and productive and informed citizens, students need to learn how to evaluate the strengths and weaknesses of someone else's arguments, how to sift fact from opinion and fallacy, and how to test the relative merits and validity of their own opinions against the known facts and the best possible available information. The landmark series Opposing Viewpoints has been providing students with just such critical-thinking skills and exposure to the debates surrounding society's most urgent contemporary issues for many years, and it continues to serve this essential role with undiminished commitment, care, and rigor.

The key to the series's success in achieving its goal of sharpening students' critical-thinking and analytic skills resides in its title—

Opposing Viewpoints. In every intriguing, compelling, and engaging volume of this series, readers are presented with the widest possible spectrum of distinct viewpoints, expert opinions, and informed argumentation and commentary, supplied by some of today's leading academics, thinkers, analysts, politicians, policy makers, economists, activists, change agents, and advocates. Every opinion and argument anthologized here is presented objectively and accorded respect. There is no editorializing in any introductory text or in the arrangement and order of the pieces. No piece is included as a "straw man," an easy ideological target for cheap point-scoring. As wide and inclusive a range of viewpoints as possible is offered, with no privileging of one particular political ideology or cultural perspective over another. It is left to each individual reader to evaluate the relative merits of each argument— as he or she sees it, and with the use of ever-growing critical-thinking skills—and grapple with his or her own assumptions, beliefs, and perspectives to determine how convincing or successful any given argument is and how the reader's own stance on the issue may be modified or altered in response to it.

This process is facilitated and supported by volume, chapter, and selection introductions that provide readers with the essential context they need to begin engaging with the spotlighted issues, with the debates surrounding them, and with their own perhaps shifting or nascent opinions on them. In addition, guided reading and discussion questions encourage readers to determine the authors' point of view and purpose, interrogate and analyze the various arguments and their rhetoric and structure, evaluate the arguments' strengths and weaknesses, test their claims against available facts and evidence, judge the validity of the reasoning, and bring into clearer, sharper focus the reader's own beliefs and conclusions and how they may differ from or align with those in the collection or those of their classmates.

Research has shown that reading comprehension skills improve dramatically when students are provided with compelling, intriguing, and relevant "discussable" texts. The subject matter of these collections could not be more compelling, intriguing, or urgently relevant to today's students and the world they are poised to inherit. The anthologized articles and the reading and discussion questions that are included with them also provide the basis for stimulating, lively, and passionate classroom debates. Students who are compelled to anticipate objections to their own argument and identify the flaws in those of an opponent read more carefully, think more critically, and steep themselves in relevant context, facts, and information more thoroughly. In short, using discussable text of the kind provided by every single volume in the Opposing Viewpoints series encourages close reading, facilitates reading comprehension, fosters research, strengthens critical thinking, and greatly enlivens and energizes classroom discussion and participation. The entire learning process is deepened, extended, and strengthened.

For all of these reasons, Opposing Viewpoints continues to be exactly the right resource at exactly the right time—when we most need to provide readers with the critical-thinking tools and skills that will not only serve them well in school but also in their careers and their daily lives as decision-making family members, community members, and citizens. This series encourages respectful engagement with and analysis of opposing viewpoints and fosters a resulting increase in the strength and rigor of one's own opinions and stances. As such, it helps make readers "future ready," and that readiness will pay rich dividends for the readers themselves, for the citizenry, for our society, and for the world at large.

Introduction

The young medic, intent on treating recently wounded soldiers in a hospital tent in Iraq, didn't hear the bomb coming. The blast knocked her to the floor. She screamed, silently in her own head, then blacked out. A few seconds later, a voice talked quietly in her ear, repeating calming words about courage and survival. She felt an arm circling her shoulders. Her panic began to recede, and her heart rate returned to normal. But wait! This was not a horrific event, she was not a terrified victim, and she was not in Iraq. Instead, the soldier was in a therapist's office, removing a virtual reality (VR) headset. She had just experienced a treatment for post-traumatic stress disorder (PTSD) using a promising new method of decreasing anxiety. Mental health care is only one of many applications of VR. Many experts believe that virtual reality is set to become one of the most pervasive technologies in the world today.

Inventors and engineers have been attempting to create virtual reality for many years. In the 1960s an inventor made an interactive theater experience called the Sensorama. Viewers sat in a dark booth on a rotating chair facing screens showing stereoscopic images. The booth had speakers for sound and devices that emitted smells. A few years later, engineers at Philco Corporation developed the first head-mounted display (HMD). It wasn't until high-performance computers were developed in the 1980s that some of the problems with early versions of VR began to be solved.

Many engineers consider creating virtual reality systems to be incredibly challenging. People's sensory organs and brains have evolved to provide a finely synchronized system. Building a VR system that simulates the real world requires assembling the correct combination of hardware, software, and sensory input. If a VR system is successful, participants feel as if they are present in the VR environment. The images in the environment appear life-sized and change as participants move around the space. If the systems are not synchronized, and there is a delay between people's actions and the systems' responses, the experience is disrupted. The participants become aware they are in an artificial environment, which then loses its real feeling.

Modern VR systems are becoming more sophisticated, comfortable, and affordable for the consumers and organizations that use them. The systems still use HMDs, though some have shrunk to the size of ski goggles. Participants also use suits, gloves, workbenches, and joysticks to augment their experiences. One of the primary—and earliest—users of VR is the U.S. military. VR is a safe, cost-effective way to train soldiers in the equipment they use in battle. VR simulations allow soldiers to learn flying skills or practice combat skills. VR is being used to treat soldiers with post-traumatic stress disorder. The VR gradually exposes soldiers to the situations that trigger their anxiety, and therapists teach them ways to cope.

Virtual reality is becoming important in other areas such as medicine, education, and business. In VR simulations, physicians can practice surgical skills. Patients have successfully used virtual reality to cope with painful treatments. Clinicians use VR to treat phobias or manage anxiety and trauma. Teachers are excited about taking students on VR field trips to places well outside their ability to visit. Professionals in real estate, architecture, engineering, travel, and sports anticipate the ways in which they can apply virtual reality to their field.

Though experts and researchers in many fields are finding beneficial uses for virtual reality, they also realize that consuming VR can have risks. Some researchers have found that behavior while in a VR world could have lasting impact after the users return to the physical world. Virtual reality is new technology, and no one knows the impact of long-term immersion. Once consumers buy their own systems, there are no limits on the time they can spend occupied in VR. Similar to obsessive internet and video game activity, some VR enthusiasts can lose their ability to control their use. They might become so involved in VR that they neglect themselves and their friends and family. Virtual reality might become a substitute for interactions in the real world.

VR content can be dangerous to users. Similar to the lists of video game content available to consumers, much of current VR content has violent, adult, or horror themes. Some experts are concerned about VR systems that place users in violent situations. Users can act as victims or perpetrators of violence with physical risk to self or others. The experts suggest that the users could become desensitized to the violence in both the VR world and in the physical world. Some VR content might reinforce undesirable personality traits that users reveal in the physical world.

Some technology professionals have concerns about privacy in a VR world. Users can reveal a great deal about their interests and preferences to anyone or any agency sharing access to the VR application. Users become a target audience to be influenced or manipulated by commercial interests that carry over to the physical world. Some VR professionals wonder if some regulations might be necessary to protect users and ensure that data collected is managed in a responsible way.

Virtual reality is an exciting and promising new technology. Though primarily developed for entertainment, VR has quickly been adapted for uses in mental health, medicine, the military, and business. While users are finding benefits in VR, they are also becoming aware of the risks. These aspects are explored in the chapters of this book: Is a Simulated World a Better World?, How Real Is Real?, What Impact Will Virtual Reality Have on Human Behavior?, and Will Virtual Reality Lead to a Decline in Society? There is much to consider as virtual reality becomes the next big technology to transform the world.

OPPOSING
VIEWPOINTS®
SERIES

CHAPTER 1

Is a Simulated World a Better World?

Chapter Preface

Avid video game players have been anticipating virtual reality applications for the last thirty years. Creating the ability to leave one's physical world and enter an imagined environment has been a goal for many engineers and game developers. The term "virtual reality" (VR) has been around since purportedly coined by inventor Jaron Lanier in 1987. The word "virtual" means "near or close, but not actual." Reality is what humans experience in the world. So virtual reality is experience that emulates reality. People normally experience their environment through sensory information, which is processed in their brains. If people are presented with made-up information, their brains could process this information as a version of reality that isn't available, but is perceived to be real. This invented reality is a three-dimensional, computer-generated environment. People can enter this environment and immerse themselves, reacting to it as if it was real.

While virtual reality might have had its start among the video gaming community, experts in other fields quickly explored the potential of VR. They wondered if the virtual environments could take the place of real environments. They wanted to test whether the behavior of soldiers, medical patients, and athletes in a virtual space could impact their behavior in physical environments. Though creating virtual reality is expensive and challenging, VR provides less risk than the real environments it replaces.

Not all experts agree, however, that virtual reality is risk free. Some developers of VR hardware and software warn consumers about the potential harmful side effects, both physical and psychological, of use and over-use of virtual reality. Some users report feelings of nausea, headache, and eye strain after using headsets. Researchers are more concerned about the effects on the mental health of VR users. They are finding that the realistic environments of virtual reality can change how users think, feel, and behave. While military and medical professionals are exploring the possibilities of this new medium, they are paying attention to long-term negative as well as positive effects. The following viewpoints explore the many considerations for those who choose to enter virtual reality.

> *"We can expect to see many more innovative uses for the technology in the future and perhaps a fundamental way in which we communicate and work thanks to the possibilities of virtual reality."*

Virtual Reality Is More Than Just Entertainment

Virtual Reality Society

In the following viewpoint, the Virtual Reality Society defines virtual reality and gives examples of its applications. Virtual reality is the development of a three-dimensional computer-generated environment that interacts with our senses to make users believe it is real. Developers are creating VR technologies that have a wide variety of applications, such as in medicine, the military, and education. The Virtual Reality Society is an information and news resource for virtual reality and related technologies

As you read, consider the following questions:

1. According to the article, how do people's real senses react to computer-generated environments?
2. What does the article mean by a VR user having a "sense of presence?"
3. What characteristics do all virtual reality systems share?

"What Is Virtual Reality," Virtual Reality Society.

The definition of virtual reality comes, naturally, from the definitions for both "virtual" and "reality." The definition of "virtual" is near and reality is what we experience as human beings. So the term "virtual reality" basically means "near-reality." This could, of course, mean anything but it usually refers to a specific type of reality emulation.

We know the world through our senses and perception systems. In school we all learned that we have five senses: taste, touch, smell, sight and hearing. These are however only our most obvious sense organs. The truth is that humans have many more senses than this, such as a sense of balance for example. These other sensory inputs, plus some special processing of sensory information by our brains ensures that we have a rich flow of information from the environment to our minds.

Everything that we know about our reality comes by way of our senses. In other words, our entire experience of reality is simply a combination of sensory information and our brains' sense-making mechanisms for that information. It stands to reason then, that if you can present your senses with made-up information; your perception of reality would also change in response to it. You would be presented with a version of reality that isn't really there, but from your perspective it would be perceived as real. Something we would refer to as a virtual reality.

So, in summary, virtual reality entails presenting our senses with a computer generated virtual environment that we can explore in some fashion.

In Technical Terms...

Answering "what is virtual reality" in technical terms is straight-forward. Virtual reality is the term used to describe a three-dimensional, computer generated environment which can be explored and interacted with by a person. That person becomes part of this virtual world or is immersed within this environment and whilst there, is able to manipulate objects or perform a series of actions.

How Is Virtual Reality Achieved?

Although we talk about a few historical early forms of virtual reality elsewhere on the site, today virtual reality is usually implemented using computer technology. There are a range of systems that are used for this purpose, such as headsets, omni-directional treadmills and special gloves. These are used to actually stimulate our senses together in order to create the illusion of reality.

This is more difficult than it sounds, since our senses and brains are evolved to provide us with a finely synchronized and mediated experience. If anything is even a little off we can usually tell. This is where you'll hear terms such asimmersiveness and realism enter the conversation. These issues that divide convincing or enjoyable virtual reality experiences from jarring or unpleasant ones are partly technical and partly conceptual. Virtual reality technology needs to take our physiology into account. For example, the human visual field does not look like a video frame. We have (more or less) 180 degrees of vision and although you are not always consciously aware of your peripheral vision, if it were gone you'd notice. Similarly when what your eyes and the vestibular system in your ears tell you are in conflict it can cause motion sickness. Which is what happens to some people on boats or when they read while in a car.

If an implementation of virtual reality manages to get the combination of hardware, software and sensory synchronicity just right it achieves something known as a sense of presence. Where the subject really feels like they are present in that environment.

Why Have Virtual Reality?

This may seems like a lot of effort, and it is! What makes the development of virtual reality worthwhile? The potential entertainment value is clear. Immersive films and video games are good examples. The entertainment industry is after all a multi-billion dollar one and consumers are always keen on novelty. Virtual reality has many other, more serious, applications as well.

WHO INVENTED VIRTUAL REALITY?

It is difficult to state with any certainty who the father of virtual reality is as like any new invention, it draws upon many different sources and influences.

More than one person has been involved in the development of this technological system but if we are talking about the realm of virtual experience then the answer is Morton Heilig.

He produced the first interactive film experience in which viewers were invited to watch a film which would use all of their senses. This multi-sensory experience was the first "3D film" which was designed for a single viewing only and enabled the viewer to become part of the film. For example: he used an oscillating fan so that the viewer could feel wind blowing on their face.

The Sensorama was not widely adopted but the ideas helped to drive future research into virtual reality and the subsequent outcomes.

Other people who lay claim to this title include:
- Jaron Lanier
- Douglas Engelbart
- Ivan Sutherland
- Myron Krueger

Jaron Lanier is credited as the person who coined the term virtual reality but there are others who worked with various aspects of this technology.

"Who Invented Virtual Reality," Virtual Reality Society.

There are a wide variety of applications for virtual reality which include:

- Architecture
- Sport
- Medicine
- The Arts
- Entertainment

Virtual reality can lead to new and exciting discoveries in these areas which impact upon our day to day lives.

Wherever it is too dangerous, expensive or impractical to do something in reality, virtual reality is the answer. From trainee fighter pilots to medical applications trainee surgeons, virtual reality allows us to take virtual risks in order to gain real world experience. As the cost of virtual reality goes down and it becomes more mainstream you can expect more serious uses, such as education or productivity applications, to come to the fore. Virtual reality and its cousin augmented reality could substantively change the way we interface with our digital technologies. Continuing the trend of humanising our technology.

Features of Virtual Reality Systems

There are many different types of virtual reality systems but they all share the same characteristics such as the ability to allow the person to view three-dimensional images. These images appear life-sized to the person.

Plus they change as the person moves around their environment which corresponds with the change in their field of vision. The aim is for a seamless join between the person's head and eye movements and the appropriate response, e.g. change in perception. This ensures that the virtual environment is both realistic and enjoyable.

A virtual environment should provide the appropriate responses—in real time—as the person explores their surroundings. The problems arise when there is a delay between the person's actions and system response or latency which then disrupts their experience. The person becomes aware that they are in an artificial environment and adjusts their behaviour accordingly which results in a stilted, mechanical form of interaction.

The aim is for a natural, free-flowing form of interaction which will result in a memorable experience.

Summary

Virtual reality is the creation of a virtual environment presented to our senses in such a way that we experience it as if we were really there. It uses a host of technologies to achieve this goal and is a technically complex feat that has to account for our perception and cognition. It has both entertainment and serious uses. The technology is becoming cheaper and more widespread. We can expect to see many more innovative uses for the technology in the future and perhaps a fundamental way in which we communicate and work thanks to the possibilities of virtual reality.

> *"Immersive virtual-reality technologies help students learn by giving them an 'inside view' of a structure or an environment ... that they might otherwise observe only externally."*

Schools Struggle with Virtual Reality

Benjamin Herold

In the following viewpoint, Benjamin Herold argues that virtual reality can give students a powerful way to learn. Some educators have used the Oculus Rift headset to provide K–12 students with virtual fieldtrips through the solar system. Universities have created virtual campus tours for prospective students. Herold warns that significant obstacles, particularly financing, will prevent widespread adoption, at least in the near future. Herold is a staff writer for Education Week.

As you read, consider the following questions:

1. According to the author, what are some of the applications of virtual reality in education?
2. According to the author, what are some of the obstacles that schools are having in implementing virtual reality?
3. What are some of the education benefits for students when schools implement virtual reality into their curriculum?

"Oculus Rift Fueling New Vision for Virtual Reality in K-12," Benjamin Herold, *Education Week*, August 26, 2014. Reprinted with permission from Editorial Projects in Education.

After decades of false starts and unkept promises, makers of virtual-reality technology could soon be ready to give students a new and potentially powerful way to learn.

In March, the social-media giant Facebook paid a whopping $2 billion to acquire Oculus VR, the Irvine, Calif.-based startup behind a new virtual-reality headset known as the Oculus Rift. Facebook founder Mark Zuckerberg described Oculus' device as a "new communications platform," akin to personal computers and mobile devices, that could have similarly far-reaching implications for gaming, entertainment, social networking, and classroom learning.

Potential educational applications include virtual field trips, immersive digital learning games and simulations, and therapeutic experiences for students with special needs.

But not everyone is buying the hype. Previous virtual-reality technologies got a lot of attention in the 1990s, and again in the early 2000s, before mostly falling flat, and public schools in the United States are not exactly known as hotbeds for nurturing emerging technologies.

"Virtual reality is super-cool, but schools are still struggling with the blocking and tackling of getting basic digital technologies in classrooms," said Trace A. Urdan, a senior analyst for Wells Fargo Securities in San Francisco who tracks digital learning investment trends.

Technical Breakthroughs

Nevertheless, some veteran observers of virtual reality are convinced that the technology's moment has finally arrived. And a handful of developers have begun creating services, such as virtual-reality college tours, for the Oculus Rift.

Oculus has made technical breakthroughs, effectively addressing some of the problems that plagued previous versions of virtual-reality technologies, while dramatically lowering production costs on devices that had cost $10,000 or more, said Jeffrey Jacobson, the director of Boston-based PublicVR, a nonprofit involved in research and software development related to virtual reality in education.

At roughly $350 per headset, the Rift—and its emerging competitors—will finally make virtual-reality devices available at a price that schools and families can afford, he said.

"People will grump and say, 'I've seen all this before.'" Mr. Jacobson said. "They're wrong. This is the dawn of consumer VR."

Oculus officials declined to be interviewed for this article.

The company's backstory, though, has quickly become the stuff of tech-industry legend.

Numerous reports describe how Oculus founder Palmer Freeman Luckey, then an 18-year old home-schooled technophile, pioneered groundbreaking new approaches to VR technology in his parents' Long Beach, Calif. garage, in part using the money he earned repairing friends' iPhones.

From there, Mr. Luckey in 2012 initiated a wildly successful Kickstarter campaign that provided the millions of dollars in revenue needed to launch his company.

The $2 billion that Oculus VR fetched from Facebook surprised even industry insiders.

For now, commercial gaming appears to be the Oculus Rift's primary use, but during an online Google Hangout hosted by the White House earlier this year, Mr. Luckey touted the device's potential classroom applications, such as immersive virtual field trips and science experiments.

"Kids don't learn best from reading a book or looking at a chalkboard," Mr. Luckey said during the online discussion. "It's going to take these things that are impossible to do today and make them a part of everyday education."

He has also suggested that the devices could be given to educational institutions for free.

So far, Oculus has not made a consumer version of the Oculus Rift publicly available, but about 75,000 prototype kits for developers are now in circulation, according to media reports.

Addressing Special Needs

Mathieu Marunczyn is among the first K-12 teachers in the world to use the device with students in a classroom.

In a telephone interview, the technology and special education instructor at the Jackson School in Victoria in Western Australia said his students—all of whom have special needs, and many of whom have some form of autism—found the Oculus Rift to be "awesome."

"Visually, it's stunning," Mr. Marunczyn said. "Everything takes on a massive scale. It just provokes and promotes a very imaginative response [from students], and ultimately that's what I want to see."

Users wearing the Oculus Rift have a wide range of vision that effectively places them not in front of a screen but inside a virtual world that is displayed to them in 3-D via two separate lenses. As a user turns his or her head, the display adjusts in real time, making it feel as though he or she is inhabiting an actual environment.

Through a high-tech series of gyroscopes, motion sensors, and algorithms that can predict a user's movements, Oculus has mostly eliminated the latency and digital blurring that left users of most previous virtual-reality technologies feeling dizzy, nauseated, or simply disappointed in the experience.

Mr. Marunczyn described the calming effect on his students of structured sessions with meditative or relaxation-oriented virtual-reality apps, such as Titans of Space, a short guided tour of planets and stars.

"[The Oculus Rift] needs to be properly and ethically researched," he said, "but I think it's going to be huge."

Mr. Jacobson of PublicVR agreed, predicting that affordable virtual-reality headsets will quickly find a niche because "there will be a few things they do better than everything else."

For example, a substantial body of research from industry and the military shows that immersive virtual-reality experiences can serve as effective training tools to help people learn to perform new tasks, Mr. Jacobson said.

"When students can see the entire interior of a space, they understand how it fits together and what it means and how it works much more readily," Mr. Jacobson said. "If it's a forest, they're there. If it's a jet engine, they have their hands in it."

Facing Barriers

But whatever the promise of a new product, any company still must find a way to overcome the well-established barriers to new-technology adoption that characterize K-12 schools, said Mr. Urdan, the market analyst.

"Facebook has more money than God, so if they want to come in and disrupt education funding protocols by pumping their own money into schools, more power to them," he said. "But I haven't seen evidence that they're willing to go that far."

Mr. Urdan chalked up talk of a potential education focus for Oculus, and the possibility of free devices being given to schools, as a public relations strategy.

"If you take these things and stick them in an all-Hispanic classroom in East Palo Alto, you'll get all kinds of heartwarming news coverage of kids with helmets on their heads checking out ancient Pompeii," he said. "Good for them, but that's not a business model."

Perhaps the most promising educational use of the new virtual-reality devices parallels their primary commercial use: digital games.

Mr. Marunczyn, for example, said he briefly began experimenting with allowing his students to construct their own virtual worlds using the popular online game Minecraft, then explore those worlds in virtual reality using the Oculus Rift—a pedagogical strategy that Mr. Jacobson deemed "educational gold."

But even there, hurdles have appeared.

Shortly after Oculus VR was acquired by Facebook, Markus Persson, the creator of Minecraft and the owner of the company that developed and released the game, posted a statement on his blog.

"I definitely want to be a part of VR, but I will not work with Facebook," he wrote. "There's nothing about their history that makes me trust them."

Companies such as YouVisit, meanwhile, are beginning to hedge their bets, developing virtual-reality tools not just for the Oculus Rift, but also for Google's new Cardboard do-it-yourself virtual-reality kit and, potentially, for the anticipated outcome of Sony's foray into virtual reality, known as Project Morpheus.

"We're exploring other platforms, because we don't know when the Rift is going to be ready," said Endri Tolka, the co-founder and chief financial officer of the New York City-based YouVisit. "But Oculus is by far the strongest and most robust [virtual-reality] platform out there."

YouVisit works with colleges and universities to build virtual campus tours for prospective students. Founded in 2009, the company began with Web-based tours. In 2010, it released its first mobile app. Just this year, it finished adapting its more than 1,000 tours for the Oculus Rift.

Students considering West Virginia University, for example, can now strap on the headset and find themselves at the 50-yard line of Mountaineer Field, in the middle of the marching band's pre-football-game routine, or looking up into stands filled with thousands of fans.

Initially, the company's plan is to develop virtual-reality tours for colleges and recruiters, who will in turn provide them to recruiters armed with the Oculus Rift at fairs and other recruitment events. Eventually, the company hopes to encourage the adoption of the devices by high school guidance counselors so that students can "visit" any college they desire from their counselor's office.

"We feel the platform is going to be very big two or three years from now," Mr. Tolka said. "We wanted to be one of the first to get on."

> "With the special goggles, they could escape the four walls of the hospital."

Virtual Reality Is Transforming Healthcare

Bertalan Mesko

In the following viewpoint, Dr. Bertalan Mesko, who calls himself the Medical Futurist, describes how virtual reality applications are creating positive effects on patients and physicians. VR allows doctors, patient families, and students to be part of an operation conducted by a skilled surgeon. Patients can reduce pain and stress by becoming immersed in a VR world. Stroke victims can use VR to speed up rehabilitation. Mesko has a Ph.D in Genomics from the University of Debrecen in Hungary.

As you read, consider the following questions:

1. According to Mesko, how can using virtual reality in health care reduce costs?
2. In what ways can the hospital experience be improved with medical VR?
3. According to the author, what are the challenges in using VR in health care?

Did you know it is possible to swim with whales in the ocean while lying on a hospital bed? Have you imagined experiencing your 74th birthday as a 20-something? Perhaps followed a risky surgery from your couch?

Medical VR is an area with fascinating possibilities. It has not just moved the imagination of science-fiction fans, but also clinical researchers and real life medical practitioners. Although the field is brand new, there are already great examples of VR having a positive effect on patients' lives and physicians' work.

1) Watching operations as if you wielded the scalpel

Did you ever wonder what is going on in an operating room? What those doctors and nurses dressed in blue or green with masks on their head are doing?

For the first time in the history of medicine, on 14 April 2016 Shafi Ahmed cancer surgeon performed an operation using a virtual reality camera at the Royal London hospital. Everyone could participate in the operation in real time through the Medical Realities website and the VR in OR app. No matter whether a promising medical student from Cape Town, an interested journalist from Seattle or a worried relative, everyone could follow through two 360 degree cameras how the surgeon removed a cancerous tissue from the bowel of the patient.

Virtual reality could elevate the teaching and learning experience in medicine to a whole new level. Today, only a few students can peek over the shoulder of the surgeon during an operation and it is challenging to learn the tricks of the trade like that. With a virtual reality camera, surgeons can stream operations globally and allow medical students to actually be there in the OR using their VR goggles.

2) Relaxing chronic patients with Medical VR

Have you ever lain down on a hospital bed counting the days until you are released? Did you, as a patient ever have the feeling that time just stops in the hospital, there is nothing to do, you miss your family and friends and you are constantly worried about your condition?

Brennan Spiegel and his team at the Cedars-Sinai hospital in Los Angeles introduced VR worlds to their patients to help them release stress and reduce pain. With the special goggles, they could escape the four walls of the hospital and visit amazing landscapes in Iceland, participate in the work of an art studio or swim together with whales in the deep blue ocean.

Spiegel says that not only can the hospital experience be improved with medical VR, but the costs of care may also be reduced. By reducing stress and pain, the length of the patient's stay in the ward or the amount of resources utilized can both be decreased.

3) Making children feel like they're at home

The experience in a hospital is even more stressful and mentally burdening for small children who miss their parents, their best buddies, their favourite blanket and generally, the soothing environment called home.

Now, a Dutch company made their dreams possible. Through a smartphone and virtual glasses, VisitU makes live contact possible with a 360 degree camera at the patient's home, school or special occasions such as a birthday celebration or a football game. Though hospitalized, young patients can relax and still enjoy their lives.

Through Medical VR, it might become easier for relatives and friends to maintain relations with their loved once in hospital care since the lengthy drives to the hospital could be spared, making room for more quality time spent together.

4) Helping physicians experience life as an elderly

Did you ever wonder how it feels like to grow old? How it feels like to not be able to lift your hand above your head? How it feels like when you've lost one of your fingers, or recover from a heart attack?

Embodied Labs created "We Are Alfred" by using VR technology to show young medical students what ageing means.

Everyone can be the hypothetical Alfred for 7 minutes, and experience how it feels like to live as a 74 year-old man with audio-visual impairments.

The developers' ultimate goal is to solve the disconnection between young doctors and elderly patients due to their huge age difference. Fostering empathy between caretakers and their charges is much easier when physicians can see things from the patients' perspectives.

5) Speeding up recovery after a stroke

For patients who survived a stroke or traumatic brain injury, time is of the essence. The earlier they start rehabilitation, the better chances they have for successfully regaining lost functions.

MindMotionPro, produced by the Swiss Mindmaze allows patients to "practice" how to lift their arms or move their fingers with the help of virtual reality. Although they might not carry out the actual movement, the app enhances attention, motivation and engagement with visual and auditory feedback. The app makes the practice of repetitive movements fun for patients. The resulting mental effort helps their traumatized nervous systems to recover much faster than lying helplessly in bed.

> "*Immersive, portable, and tailor-made for the Xbox generation, these simulations are being used to do everything from treating post-traumatic stress disorder to familiarizing a soldier with an enemy base.*"

VR Helps Create Better Soldiers and Commanders

David Kushner

In the following viewpoint, David Kushner describes the ways in which the U.S. military is using virtual reality to train battle-ready soldiers and their leaders. Using VR headsets, soldiers participate in training exercises and interrogations. They learn important decision-making skills and learn to cope with the stress of battle. According to Kushner, VR is a low-risk cost effective way to train soldiers for the rigors of war. Kushner is a contributing editor for IEEE Spectrum.

"*Ender's Game* Is Already a Reality for the U.S. Military," David Kushner, *IEEE Spectrum,* October 31, 2013. Reprinted by permission.

As you read, consider the following questions:

1. According to Kushner, what are some advantages in using virtual reality simulations in military training?

2. What does Randal Hill, executive director of Institute of Creative Technologies, mean by the "human factor" in military training?

3. What does Kushner predict will be the military training of the future?

G uy with a gun right there!" shouts Army Staff Sgt. Dustin Hill, as we storm an enemy compound in Afghanistan.

Dressed in camouflage and weighed down with a backpack, I crouch with another soldier, Staff Sgt. Edwin Lopez, near a small concrete wall. I peer around the corner to see a Taliban fighter aiming at us from the doorway of a run-down two-story building. As bullets zip past my helmet, I look up into the bright blue sky to see a column of thick black smoke twisting up from a nearby rooftop. But before I can raise the heavy rifle in my hands, I hear the scream of a bullet, and everything goes black.

As someone helps me take off my helmet, I'm suddenly not in Afghanistan anymore. Motion-tracking sensors are strapped to my arms and legs. My backpack holds a computer processing unit. Virtual reality goggles dangle from my helmet. The gun in my hands is an exact replica of an M16—except for the tiny joystick on the back of the trigger to control my motion.

I'm in a convention center in Orlando, Fla., at the Interservice/Industry Training, Simulation and Education Conference, the largest military simulation conference in the world. And I've just experienced the Army's most lifelike training simulation yet: the Dismounted Soldier Training System which, after two years and US $57 million in development, will arrive at bases this year.

Yes, it's the stuff of science fiction, most notably *Ender's Game*, the best-selling 1985 novel by Orson Scott Card that has whiz-kid cadets fighting an alien space fleet through a video game (the book was based on a short story by Card of the same name, published in 1977 as *Analog Science Fiction and Fact*). Among military geeks, the book—which is being officially released as a $100 mission film starring Harrison Ford and Ben Kingsley on 1 November—has been a blueprint for the future for years. As Michael Macedonia, the former director of the Army's simulation technology center told *The New York Times* in 2003, "*Ender's Game* has had a lot of influence on our thinking. The intent is to build a simulation that allows people to play in that world for months or years, participate in different types of roles, and see consequences of their decisions."

Ten years later, Macedonia's vision is bearing fruit, driven in part by a strong appetite for the savings that simulations promise in a time of tight budgets. The University of Southern California Institute for Creative Technologies (ICT) is a U.S. government–funded research and development organization in Playa Vista, Calif., that makes some of the most convincing military simulations around. According to ICT, one of its training tools, the Joint Fires and Effects Training System, saved the military $3 million per year on what the fuel would have cost for the comparable training with real vehicles. And according to a recent report in *National Defense* magazine, the Air Force "estimates it could save about $1.7 billion over five years by reducing flying hours by 5 percent and shifting more of its pilot and crew training to simulators."

The technology has also been buoyed by consumer trends. Although simulations have been used in the military for decades, advances in mobile devices and computer graphics cards are helping sims replace live training for a wider range of roles than ever before, both on and off the battlefield.

Officers refine counseling and interrogation skills on artificially intelligent virtual humans. Commanders execute complex battle drills as if they were a giant round of *World of Warcraft*. Soldiers dispose of improvised explosive devices in driving simulators. Immersive, portable, and tailor-made for the Xbox generation, these simulations are being used to do everything from treating post-traumatic stress disorder to familiarizing a soldier with an enemy base, as in the case of the Afghanistan scenario I experienced.

"We don't give them a manual, we don't send them home for three weeks to study," says James Blake, head of the U.S. Army Program Executive Office for Simulation, Training and Instrumentation. "We just put them in the environment, put the device on them, and exercise."

Once Upon a Time

The use of video games for military training began in 1980. *Battlezone*, a popular arcade hit that pitted players against three-dimensional (albeit wireframe) tanks, was modified for the Army to school Bradley Fighting Vehicle gunners. But when he was writing the *Ender's Game* short story and novel, Card didn't find much in his neighborhood arcade to inspire a vision for the virtual warriors of the future. "None of the games I had seen were remotely useful in preparing soldiers for either combat or leadership," he says.

So he imagined the Battle School, and the simulated training environment that dominates the latter part of *Ender's Game* (earlier in the narrative, training is conducted mostly in a series of rooms in which the cadets physically engage in zero-gravity combat). The book's young hero, Ender Wiggin, proves himself an expert war gamer, masterfully maneuvering first his own digital fleet and then a fleet of fleets commanded by other students against an enemy race of alien "buggers." The training program is ruthless and unrelenting, driving Ender to invent tactic after tactic. The Battle School became a paradigm of just how convincing simulations can be.

Today, the U.S. Army is leading the fight to bring such simulations to life, nowhere more than at the ICT. Spread out over an office park and launched by the Army in 1999 under the auspices of USC, the ICT leverages talent from the movie and video-game industries in nearby Hollywood [for insight into ICT's early years, see "Games Soldiers Play," *IEEE Spectrum*, March 2002].

The Institute now employs over 180 game developers, filmmakers, artists, and engineers, and it gets half of its $35 million annual budget from the Army. The other half comes from customers such as the Department of Defense and the Navy. Pocket change compared to the budget of many defense programs (the development of just the engine of the F-35 Joint Strike Fighter plane has been budgeted at $4 billion), ICT's budget is evidence that simulation technology can provide a lot of bang for the buck. Nonetheless, the ICT is facing flat or decreasing funding levels due to defense cuts.

Visiting the ICT feels like going to an *Ender's Game* version of Willy Wonka's factory. Upstairs in a darkened room, a young man sits inside something called a Light Stage. A camera on a rotating arm around an actor captures a perfectly rendered, 3-D digital version of him, which will later be animated and incorporated into training simulations. (The technology has also been used in films such as *Avatar* and *Spider-Man 2*.) Paul Debevec, who did visual effects for *The Matrix* before becoming the ICT's associate director of graphics research, calls the results "virtual humans."

Downstairs in another studio, I get to interact with one of the ICT's virtual soldiers in the Emergent Leader Immersive Training Environment (ELITE) system. The system has been deployed at facilities such as the Maneuver Center of Excellence at Fort Benning, Ga., and the Officer Training Command Newport.

The purpose of this war game is to train officers in counseling skills. Sitting before a large computer monitor, I see a life-size, lifelike camouflaged staff sergeant on screen fidgeting in a chair in a small cluttered office. I'm told he has been having conflict with his platoon sergeant. "It's all good," the virtual man tells me, when I ask how things are going on base. "It's not all good," I reply, choosing from three lines of possible dialogue on a small screen beside me. "Fix the attitude with your platoon sergeant."

After completing my counseling session, I receive my evaluation from the computer program. A softer approach, I learn, would have gleaned me more information about the sergeant's conflict.

The ICT's creation and deployment of virtual humans serves several purposes. First, it's cheaper: Hiring real-life role players is both expensive and limiting (only so many soldiers, after all, can interact with a real person at a time). Second, it's part of what the Army has categorized as "the human dimension." Randall Hill Jr., executive director of the ICT, says that in the past the military's view on technology would "often focus on how you buy equipment and treat the soldier like a Christmas tree: hang armor on him and gadgets and not look at them holistically." Now the Army uses technology to empower soldiers more as humans, not mere weapons carriers. "We're trying to look at soldiers that way," says Hill. "Our research into virtual humans plays well into that element of training."

Julia Kim, an ICT project director who is a developing a counterterrorist intelligence training game for the Naval Post Graduate School, distances the ICT's work from the violence of the simulations in *Ender's Game*. "From a moral perspective I have profound issues with *Ender's Game*," she says, noting that her goal is not to turn soldiers into killing machines but rather equip them with survival skills. "*Ender's Game* presents an ethical framework that is problematic," she adds.

For his part, Card lauds the efforts of institutions such as the ICT to better equip the next generation of Americans entering warfare. He also cautions against using the book as a blueprint for how to desensitize the Enders of tomorrow to combat. "If, to any degree, *Ender's Game* has helped the U.S. military to train its soldiers more effectively and to reduce both the dangers and economic costs of war, then I rejoice in that good effect," he says. "However, my purpose in writing was to tell a story, and the primary effect of storytelling is behavioral: The story, once it dwells in the memory of the audience, helps shape the community's view of which motives and actions are important, and, of the important ones, which are admirable and which despicable."

VR Domes Assess Soldier's Thinking

It's not the Star Trek holodeck but a computer-generated reality "dome" in Massachusetts should immerse war fighters in a virtual environment that not only tests their skills, but allows Army researchers to assess soldier cognitive abilities.

The virtual reality dome is the creation of researchers at the U.S. Army Natick Soldier Research, Development and Engineering Center, where a Cognitive Science and Applications Team hopes to study the impact of real-world operational situations on decision-making, spatial memory and way finding.

The simulations will be modeled on real-world locations.

"The integration of multiple input modalities, along with multisensory feedback, increases the realism, immersion and engagement on behalf of users subjected to prolonged, workload-intensive activities," cognitive science team leader Dr. Caroline Mahoney said.

The dome is a concave virtual-reality system that provides a full 180-degree horizontal field, using high-density, front-projection to create a high-resolution, visual world.

Other scientists at the Natick lab are developing metrics for measuring cognitive workload during mission tasks. This will enable researchers to assess how new equipment and technology born by soldiers effects their cognitive abilities, according to Mahoney.

The data from those measurements will eventually help in the design and development of soldier technology and equipment by center researchers and outside equipment manufacturers.

"Virtual Reality Dome to Assess Soldier Thinking in Virtual Combat Environment," Bryant Jordan, March 18, 2016.

Training Armies

Shortly after completing my simulated combat at the military conference in Orlando, I join my virtual war buddies, Hill and Lopez, in a small back room to discuss the experience. Dressed in real camouflage, their replica M16s resting against the wall, the two seem weary from several days demonstrating the Dismounted Soldier Training System. While organizations like the ICT spend millions creating war games, the application of the systems ultimately falls on drill sergeants such as these two.

Hill, a stoic 29-year-old with a fuzzy brown crew cut, and Lopez, an affable 27-year-old from Rhode Island, are lifelong gamers, just like the young enlistees they train to become soldiers at Fort Benning. Over the past decade, the Army has distributed a free online video game for personal computers, *America's Army*, as a recruitment tool. But when recruits arrive at Fort Benning they have to check their flashy first-person-shooter skills—typically learned in more gung-ho video-game titles—at the door.

"We get kids who come in with unrealistic views of the Army because of Call of Duty," Hill says, referring to Activision Blizzard's popular video game franchise. "You're not going to come in here and run around like you're in a one-man war."

Down the hall at the trade show, I previewed *Virtual Battle Space 3* or *VBS3*, an upcoming sequel to the most widely used tactical training video game in the Army: Earlier versions are used on more than 70 bases (a variety of software licenses and tools are available at costs between $500 to $30 000). Though the game bears a resemblance to *Call of Duty*, with its brigade of pixelated soldiers infiltrating a dusty Middle Eastern village, the missions have a different purpose. "It's teaching people how to think," says Peter Morrison, the young CEO of the game's Orlando-based developer, Bohemia Interactive Simulations. "You're not using the game to teach people how to shoot."

VBS3 is a virtual sandbox that can be used to create training exercises on the fly. The software contains thousands of vehicles, terrains, weapons, and characters. Using a mission-editing program, a commander can stage millions of possible scenarios for a trainee to navigate.

Morrison demonstrates it for me. With a few clicks of his mouse, he drops some palm trees and buildings in a small town. "Now we'll choose our IED," he says, dragging an explosive soft drink can into the dirt. With another click and drag, he places a squad of soldiers on the street, as well as an African man in a

T-shirt and jeans. In under a minute, he has created a scenario for a trainee: Find and disarm the IED before the civilian stumbles on it accidentally and dies.

Rehearsing missions in virtual environments saves not just money but time, says Blake. "It's just like an amusement park," he says. "We want a rich enough tool set so a commander giving a task can say, 'I want some of this, some of this, and some of this, and I'd like the training next week.' "

The Army has just begun rolling out its most ambitious mission simulation project yet. Costing $27 million to develop and $490 per system to deploy, the Integrated Training Environment is a suite of government off-the-shelf hardware and software tools that allow a commander to combine virtual humans and real brigades together in what Blake calls a "blended environment." A group of live soldiers on the ground could practice attacking a target on the grounds of a military base while they're under mortar fire from a virtual enemy infantry division. The computer-generated soldiers behave realistically according to the behavioral parameters in the software. Though the live soldiers can't see the virtual troops, they are visible to commanders and the actions in the exercises of the real and virtual troops can affect each other: During live training, soldiers use a system called I-Miles, which tracks their location, uses laser tagging to simulate gunshots and note hits, and can also notify soldiers that they have, for example, been "killed" by a mortar round. Crews operating helicopter and tank simulators in training facilities can also be added to the mix.

So instead of having a single brigade of, say, 20 soldiers in a field, a commander can have three giant brigades with tanks, helicopters, and air strikes—quickly and cheaply. Because the overhead action—from live troop positions, crews in vehicle simulators, and virtual units—is all displayed on the same computer screen, commanders get a bird's-eye view that blurs the line between what's real and what's not.

But no matter how sophisticated a simulation becomes, or how convincing a virtual human, it has one fundamental limitation:

"You can't get the emotions from it," as Dustin Hill tells me. "You don't get the emotions from your battle buddy being shot."

Beyond *Ender's Game*

To get a glimpse of where our war games are going in the future, I head to the Mixed Reality Lab at the ICT. The lab is a giant, black-draped studio filled with the latest, greatest virtual reality gear. A rack of VR suits—used to track one's body in a simulated environment—hangs on one wall. On another side, I slip on a giant red helmet and find myself inside a bright, vivid Afghanistan with a Humvee so realistic I step out of the way to avoid smacking into the fender.

When I slip off the gear, my eyes toggle back to reality, and a spry man in thick-framed black glasses is standing before me: the Willy Wonka of virtual reality himself, Mark Bolas. A pioneering engineer in VR since the 1980s, Bolas has a copy of *Ender's Game* on his desk, but he says the book now feels dated. "I almost think it's passé at this point," he says. "*Ender's Game* is happening. It's already done."

Bolas leads me past the rack of VR body suits, which can immerse a person's entire body into a VR world. The suits have sensors that allow a virtual avatar to match the posture of a wearer. (Bolas is also experimenting with a Kinect sensor, the motion-capturing device developed for the Xbox 360, to detect the basic geometry of the wearer.) Tracking gestures in this way "provides the ability to see one's own body in the environment," Bolas says, "This is very important. If a user reaches out his or her hand or looks down at their feet, it is disconcerting not to see anything."

He leads me to another area and hands me a small black cardboard box, into which I peer. Pressing my eyes against the viewfinder, I see a deep red desert landscape. But this isn't a virtual Afghanistan; it's Mars, created from pictures gathered from NASA probes. After hearing me marvel at the fidelity, Bolas effectively pulls the rabbit from the hat, reaching into the black box to reveal an iPhone with a Retina display. The box is a small, foldable viewer that collapses flat enough to be shipped in a manila envelope. Created with the help of students and researchers at the USC School of Cinematic Arts, the device is called FOV2GO and exemplifies the cheap and increasingly mobile new wave of off-the-shelf virtual reality hardware.

Bolas predicts that within a few years, a young soldier will be sitting in, say, California in a VR headset and navigating a drone halfway across the world. "Instead of having to go somewhere in the desert and do training and get deployed," he says, "you just download the environment you're going to go into, maybe with data they just took yesterday, and all of a sudden you're really going through that environment." Bolas calls this "just-in-time training."

In fact, it seems Bolas is right about *Ender's Game* actually being old news. Even as the movie hits screens, it will have to contend with a reality that's already leaving the fantasy behind. Still, author Card cautions against putting too much stock in war games, no matter how impressive they become.

"Engineers and programmers change the playing field by constantly advancing the means of offense and defense," he tells me, "But Ender Wiggin and his ilk take these tools and figure out ways to use them under combat conditions. In a sense, the tools do not matter; that is, whatever the tools are the great commanders figure out new ways to use them…. It remains true, in the real world as in *Ender's Game*, that there is no military component more important than the quality of command."

> *"One question his project aims to answer is whether students learn as well in VR as they do in real classrooms."*

Virtual Reality Can Revolutionize Higher Education

David Matthews

In the following viewpoint, David Matthews reports on the ways academics in higher education are using virtual reality to increase educational options for university students. Engineering and architecture students can use VR to design and manipulate virtual structures. One challenge is to determine if students learn as well in the VR world as in the physical world. Matthews is a higher education reporter covering research and science.

As you read, consider the following questions:

1. In what ways have universities used virtual reality technology to increase the learning of students?
2. What are some of the challenges educators face in adapting virtual reality for classrooms and labs?
3. According to Matthews, how do students react to using VR as part of their university curriculum?

"Virtual Reality: Could It Revolutionize Higher Education?" David Matthews, *The Times Higher Education*, June 2, 2016.

In *Ready Player One*, perhaps the best known novel yet written about virtual reality (VR), the protagonist Wade Watts lives in a cramped trailer, scavenges for food and has to dodge murderers and rapists on a bleak and dangerous compound on the outskirts of Oklahoma City.

Yet although he lives in a dystopian vision of the world in 2044, the teenage Wade in some ways has access to a better education than any young person today.

Because he can plug into a wildly popular, hyper-realistic virtual world called the OASIS, Wade is able to attend a virtual school where teachers take their classes on astonishing field trips: they go inside the human heart to watch how it pumps blood around the body; they witness archaeologists discover Tutankhamen's tomb; or they stand on the volcanic surface of Jupiter's moon Io to observe the planet's Great Red Spot.

His teachers, also logged in to the virtual world, are highly motivated, largely because they can effectively mute pupils' avatars to prevent any bad behaviour.

VR has long been a staple of science fiction. But this year sees the release of several consumer headsets that are advanced enough to fool users' unconscious minds into believing that they really are in another world—something called "presence" in the jargon of the industry—and largely eliminate the nausea that plagued earlier products in the 1990s.

At first, these headsets (which range from ultra-basic cardboard models to £700 kits, and are powered by smartphones, games consoles and desktop computers) seem destined to be used largely for a hedonistic mix of gaming, virtual cinema and pornography.

But a handful of academics are exploring how they can be used to teach students.

The most obvious use of VR is in subjects such as engineering or architecture, where headset-wearing students can design and manipulate virtual structures. Conrad Tucker, an assistant professor of engineering at Pennsylvania State University, has received funding to build a virtual engineering lab where students hold, rotate and fit together virtual parts as they would with their real hands.

"What we want to do now is get down to the nuts and bolts," he tells *Times Higher Education*, and allow students to do things such as use screws and hammers in VR as they would in real life.

Technology to simulate physically realistic environments—where objects drop and bounce as you would expect them to—has already been developed, he explains. "You have the gaming industry to thank for this," he adds.

It is even possible to build a car out of virtual components and have it run based on laws of physics modelled into the environment, Tucker adds.

One question his project aims to answer is whether students learn as well in VR as they do in real classrooms, or whether without being physically present with their classmates, they miss out on developing intangible skills such as teamwork. "We really don't know what level of immersion can be achieved in this virtual environment," he says.

This new generation of VR headsets is only just hitting the market, so schools and universities have not had long to assess them. However, according to a meta-analysis published in 2014, students at school and university do learn better when they are immersed in virtual worlds.

The same year saw the University of British Columbia experiment with a full lecture in VR. Five students were given an earlier version of the Oculus Rift headset and sat in a virtual classroom where they watched a gaming lawyer deliver a lecture (his movements were captured with a camera, so that his virtual avatar moved just like him in real life—although his movements were apparently a little "funky"). His slides appeared on a virtual screen behind his avatar.

The students were overwhelmingly positive and felt that even this prototype set-up was an effective way to attend a lecture. However, there was one big problem—with headsets covering their entire field of view, the students were unable to take notes in the real world.

Virtual environments help students memorise material better because "you activate more of your brain because…it's not a single channel [sense]," says Xavier Fouger, senior director at Dassault Systèmes, a company that makes 3D models and simulations. This way all students, whether they learn best visually, or through touch or hearing, will be stimulated, he argues.

Dassault Systèmes has already built virtual reality models of the Mulberry harbours used in the D-Day landings, and collaborated with Harvard University to create a 3D model of the ancient Egyptian Giza Plateau. Students can peer into now-inaccessible tombs recreated from sketches and photos made by the archaeologists who unearthed them.

But the use of VR in humanities subjects such as English and history may be more limited and controversial than in the likes of engineering.

For a start, the bulk of these students' time is spent analysing texts. It is unclear exactly what VR would add to reading *Beowulf*.

There is also a risk that in "recreating a lost building, for example, you might give users the idea that the virtual reality model is what really existed, though the reconstruction might be only hypothetical", says Glenn Gunhouse, a senior lecturer in art history at Georgia State University.

Gunhouse, who has recreated a virtual version of the ancient Egyptian Tomb of Menna that his students tour using an Oculus Rift headset, thinks that one way to solve this would be to "allow users to toggle between modes, hiding and then revealing the reconstructed parts."

He hopes to kit out an entire computer lab with Rifts, although this will not be cheap—the headset and powerful computers required to run high-end VR currently start at about £1,700 combined. But Tucker points out that this is not too far off what students might be expected to spend on textbooks.

Still, for the moment, the future of VR rests on how well it succeeds with gamers, rather than lecturers. "I hope it doesn't become the next fad," Tucker says. "If it fails in the entertainment industry, it could not gain traction in education, which would be a shame."

Despite the obvious potential in some areas of higher education, no one *THE* spoke to thought that VR would somehow replace the physical campus, as it has for Wade Watts.

It could, however, help universities to optimise their use of space, reserving real labs for when they are truly needed. "Maybe repetitive tasks in a physical lab could be done in virtual reality," says Tucker.

Then there is the question of whether students doing much of their degree in VR would miss out on the all-important social side of university. Tucker points out that the vast majority of students' time is not spent in classes—and this time is crucial to their overall experience—although Gunhouse thinks that students may ultimately be able to have genuine social interactions in VR.

"Online, I didn't have a problem talking to people or making friends," Wade says of himself in *Ready Player One*. But, he says, in real life "I was a painfully shy, awkward kid, with low self-esteem and almost no social skills—a side effect of spending most of my childhood inside the OASIS."

Periodical and Internet Sources Bibliography

The following articles have been selected to supplement the diverse views presented in this chapter.

Kate Abrosimova, "5 Ways Virtual Reality Will Change Education," Hypergrid Business, September 7, 2014.

Mindi Chahal, "Why 2016 Will Be Virtual Reality's Breakthrough Year," *Marketing Week*, January 28, 2016.

Brad Grossman, "Virtual Reality Is Not Just for Entertainment Anymore; How It Will Improve Health Care," *Medical Daily*, April 3, 2016.

Julia Haskins, "How Virtual Reality Is Gaining Traction in Healthcare," *Healthline*, June 15, 2016.

Sinom Parkin, "How VR Is Training the Perfect Soldier," *Wareable*, December 31, 2015.

Elizabeth Reede and Larissa Bailiff, "When Virtual Reality Meets Education," *Tech Crunch*, January 23, 2016.

Alex Senson, "Virtual Reality in Healthcare: Where's the Innovation?" *Tech Crunch*, September 16, 2015.

Bryan Sinclair and Glenn Gunhouse, "The Promise of Virtual Reality in Higher Education," *Educase Review,* March 7, 2016.

Jennifer Snelling, "Virtual Reality in K-12 Education: How Helpful Is It?" Converge, July 28, 2016.

Robert Stone, "Military Needs a More Realistic Approach to Virtual Reality," *Phys.org*, June 2, 2016.

Audrey Watters, "(Marketing) Virtual Reality in Education: A History," *Hacked Education*, July 2, 2016.

OPPOSING
VIEWPOINTS®
SERIES

CHAPTER 2

|How Real Is Real?

Chapter Preface

What would it be like, the engineers at BeAnotherLab wondered, to swap bodies with someone very different than themselves? Would this experience allow someone to virtually walk in another's shoes, see the world through his or her eyes? At the lab, using VR headsets, male participants experience what it is like to be female. Native residents develop understanding about the lives of new refugees seeking asylum. The purpose of this lab is to use VR technology to help develop empathy in people. Experiencing the perspectives of other cultures is only one of the many uses that VR developers are finding for this innovative technology.

VR engineers in labs all over the world are working hard to make virtual reality as close to physical reality as possible. They use the term "immersion" to describe the success of the technology to make users feel as if their virtual world is real. The engineers are figuring out ways to incorporate more of human senses. Users not only see a different reality, they hear, smell, and even touch in a virtual world. VR developers use the term "presence" to describe the subjective feelings and beliefs of the users when they are immersed in the VR world. Virtual reality is getting closer to the experience of physical environments.

The willingness of users to suspend their disbelief and enter a VR world is useful for VR developers in many contexts. In one experiment, physicians used VR to treat burn victims in a hospital. Changing the dressings is one of the most painful treatments burn patients experience. Doctors use VR headsets to transport the patients to a world of their choice, and the treatment is completed, pain free. VR technology is advancing at a rapid rate and more leaders in different fields are capitalizing on its ability to blur the difference between real and virtual.

As virtual reality gets closer to physical reality, some people are voicing their concerns. VR users are able to manipulate their virtual reality to create an idealized avatar and life for themselves.

Some people wonder if users might prefer their virtual world to the reality of the physical world. It might become harder for some users to stay grounded and focused on the world they have rather than the one they create. The viewpoints in this chapter present varying opinions on the blending of the real and the simulated in virtual reality.

> "A chemist could step inside a drug
> to understand it on the cellular level;
> an architect could walk through a
> building she's designing."

Virtual Reality Is Moving in Positive Directions

Maria Konnikova

In the following viewpoint, Maria Konnikova argues that virtual reality is advancing in mostly positive directions. Standing on Mars, scuba diving the Great Barrier Reef, conducting brain surgery, virtually attending and recording a family gathering are all potential applications of VR technology. She warns about unintended consequences such as the impact on users' health. Konnikova is a contributing writer for the New Yorker.

As you read, consider the following questions:

1. According to Konnikova, what are some of the potential uses that VR developers are creating for consumers?
2. How are developers incorporating sensory experiences into virtual reality?
3. According to the author, what are some of the unintended consequences that may occur as consumers use virtual reality applications?

In 1965, Ivan Sutherland, a computer-graphics pioneer, addressed an international meeting of techies on the subject of virtual reality. The ultimate virtual-reality display, he told the audience, would be "a room within which the computer can control the existence of matter. A chair displayed in such a room would be good enough to sit in. Handcuffs displayed in such a room would be confining, and a bullet displayed in such a room would be fatal. With appropriate programming, such a display could literally be the Wonderland into which Alice walked."

Virtual reality has advanced rapidly in the past couple of years—the much-anticipated Oculus Rift headset is expected to arrive in stores in early 2016, followed closely by several other devices. Yet the technology is still very new, and Sutherland's vision seems little closer to, well, actual reality. "Right now, it's like when you first had cellphones," Richard Marks, one of the lead engineers working on Project Morpheus, Sony's virtual-reality headset, told me. "A lot of focus is still on the most-basic things."

I recently spoke with scientists, psychologists, engineers, and developers about the possibilities for this emerging field. Where might it eventually take us—and will that be somewhere we want to go?

Being Virtually Anywhere

During a recent demonstration of Google Cardboard—a DIY headset that's made of cardboard and uses a Smartphone for the display—I found myself by turns atop a rocky peak, in a barn next to a snorting horse, and on a gondola making my way up a mountain. The gondola ride gave me vertigo.

We react like that, experts say, because our brains are easily fooled when what we see on a display tracks our head movements. "We have a reptilian instinct that responds as if it's real: Don't step off that cliff; this battle is scary," Jeremy Bailenson, the founding director of Stanford's Virtual Human Interaction Lab, told me. "The brain hasn't evolved to tell you it's not real."

Much of the excitement about virtual reality has come from the gaming community. Who wouldn't want to experience a game so completely? But gaming is just the start. At Sony, Marks has worked with NASA to conjure the experience of standing on Mars—a view that could help scientists better understand the planet. David Laidlaw, the head of the Visualization Research Lab at Brown University, told me that his team has re-created a temple site in Petra, Jordan, enabling researchers to see previously unclear relationships between objects found there.

Google is testing Expeditions, a way of sending students to places like the Great Barrier Reef, where they can virtually scuba dive as part of a lesson on marine biology and ocean acidification. Similar approaches may enhance professional training. By donning a pair of goggles, a neurosurgeon could navigate brain structures before surgery; a chemist could step inside a drug to understand it on the cellular level; an architect could walk through a building she's designing.

Another possibility: Imagine that you're unable to attend a family gathering. With a pair of glasses, you're in the middle of the action. And everyone there wears glasses that make it appear as though you're present. The whole thing is recorded, so you can replay the experience whenever you'd like. Ten years from now, such a scenario might be common.

And consider the potential for telecommuting. Henry Fuchs, a professor at the University of North Carolina at Chapel Hill and a leader in the field, envisions virtual offices. You could use the physical space of your house—a real desk, a real computer—but interact with your colleagues as if they were in the same room as you.

Seeing Through Others' Eyes

In his lab at Stanford, Bailenson studies how virtual reality changes behavior. He's found that if your avatar is taller than you are in real life, you become more confident. If you have a particularly attractive avatar, you become friendlier. If you're young and you have an avatar that is a senior citizen, you save more money. These changes last even after you leave the virtual realm.

And avatars could soon become more convincing. Most commercial virtual-reality systems capture only the movement of your head and hands. In 2013, though, Apple acquired PrimeSense, an Israeli company developing technology to track the movements of your whole body with infrared sensors and special microchips. And a company called Faceshift is working to capture facial expressions, so that if you smile or roll your eyes, your avatar will too.

Virtual reality has already proved useful in treating phobias and PTSD. It can help people overcome a fear of heights, for example, through simulations of standing on a balcony or walking across a bridge. Bailenson and others think it could also be used to build empathy. What if you could step inside a documentary, rather than just watching it on a screen—almost literally walking in someone else's shoes? That was the goal of *Clouds Over Sidra*, a virtual-reality film—created through a partnership between the United Nations and Samsung—that followed a 12-year-old girl in a Syrian-refugee camp in Jordan.

And what if you could do something similar in real time? "Combine this sort of immersive storytelling, as it evolves, with technologies like Periscope and Meerkat"—apps that let users stream live video—"and you can in essence see the world through anyone's eyes," Clay Bavor, the head of Google's virtual-reality initiatives, told me. A protester in Cairo or Athens or Baltimore, for example, could use a special camera to give people around the world a 360-degree view of what it's like to be there.

Engaging All Your Senses

Google recently acquired Thrive Audio, a company that specializes in spatial audio—sounds that your ear registers as emanating from a particular place. A virtual waterfall grows louder as you move toward it. Something catches your ear from behind. You turn, and

Virtual Reality Is Not Real World

Instead of using real and virtual to refer to the distinction, it was proposed that we should refer to them as meat-space and cyber-space, so as to put them on a more linguistically even level...

An interesting point was made that humans have been using various cyber-worlds for millennia, counting books, plays, art, and even further back to oral tradition and religions or mythologies. Escapism is an essential part of being human, biologically built into the human experience as dreams. Whether escaping into a book or a video game, it's the same root concept.

The only problem comes when it becomes difficult for the escapee to tell the difference between the cyber-world and the meat-world. One example was of someone who drove into pedestrians, thinking they were still playing Grand Theft Auto. Problems arise when people can't tell the difference between fact and fiction, and live in their own reality unshared by the rest of society.

Perhaps if everyone were able to transition into a cyber-world and leave the meat-world behind for good, then it would be acceptable, as there would still be a shared reality within the cyber-world, and no transition problems moving from one to the other.

"Cyber-space Provides Inauthentic Analog for Real World Life," Thatcher Montgomery, *The Tartan*, April 11, 2014.

see a deer approaching. The audio becomes three-dimensional, truly surrounding you.

Smell could become part of the virtual experience as well. A company called Feelreal has developed a mask that releases scents, such as the smell of fire or the ocean, to enhance what you see in a headset. (The project is hampered by the need to preload the scents you're likely to encounter, among other problems.) Closely related is the ability to taste what you see. Researchers in Singapore are developing electrodes that, when placed on your tongue, mimic basic tastes, such as sweet, salty, bitter, and sour.

What about touch? Could we one day find that when we dip our fingers in virtual water, it actually feels wet? David Laidlaw considers resolving this challenge, known as the haptics problem, to be the holy grail of virtual reality. But that doesn't mean it's insurmountable. "I'm confident we'll do it within our lifetimes," Palmer Luckey, the founder of Oculus, told me. "There are no fundamental physical laws that prevent us from building something that's almost perfect." Laidlaw is less optimistic—he thinks that creating lifelike haptics will take 100 years—but he agrees that a virtual world may one day be a nearly perfect simulacrum of the real one.

Of course, there could be unintended consequences. Already people are developing vision problems and vitamin D deficiencies—not to mention obesity and diabetes—because they spend too much time in front of screens. (See "The Nature Cure.") What might a flawlessly rendered virtual world mean for our health?

A Neuromancer Future?

Jeremy Bailenson was inspired to work in virtual reality in part by *Neuromancer*, a 1984 novel that depicts a future in which people can "jack in" their brains directly to a virtual world. Perhaps, Bailenson speculates, that's where virtual reality is headed. He imagines that in 50 or 100 years we might develop a brain-machine interface that taps directly into the nervous system.

> *"Between our tactile senses that remind us there's a couple pounds of plastic strapped to our head, and this phantom sense of a controller we feel but can't see, there's a great cognitive dissonance that prevents it from being a seamless experience."*

Virtual Reality Is Not Ready for Widespread Use

Mark Ceb

In the following viewpoint, Mark Ceb argues that virtual reality is not living up to the expectations of those who anticipated sophisticated and realistic experiences from the new technology. He compares the failure of VR to the failure of Google Glass, which was hyped by the media but failed to catch on with the public. He claims that VR hardware is too bulky for personal use and VR software is lacking. Ceb is a writer, illustrator, and video game reviewer.

"Virtual Reality or Virtual Fad?" Mark Ceb, October 28, 2015. Reprinted by permission.

As you read, consider the following questions:

1. What does Ceb mean by the "derealization and depersonalization" that VR causes in many users?
2. According to Ceb, in what ways does the development of VR compare to the development of Google Glass?
3. What does the author think are the solutions to the problems with the development of VR applications?

Yes, This Is What You Look Like

The future never quite works out as promised. Science fiction correctly predicted a few things like wearable, lightweight communicators and data pads with instant access to immeasurable libraries of information. Unfortunately, we still don't have flying cars or jet packs. Well, guess what? Virtual Reality is happening!

That's right. Suck that down, reality! We don't need you—we're making VIRTUAL reality. It's like normal reality but NEW and you have to pay for it in installments!

Do we need virtual reality? Is it enjoyable or even practical?

If I had to make some wild speculations (and who doesn't love those?), I would say it's not. Happening, that is. Like Sonic the Hedgehog I think VR in its current form needs to move into the background until a brilliant designer or the technology can tackle these outmoded ideas.

Appeal

If you want people to get on board for an idea, it has to have appeal. Outside of the Starship Enterprise's Holodeck or the Matrix, Virtual Reality has never really seemed cool. It might have seemed cool in the way that wearing ill-fitting, color-clashing outfits are cool, but that's mostly just the opinion of "ironic" hipsters. The common video games consumer doesn't see the appeal of something so niche.

To understand why it seems so niche we need to unpack the concept for its history, signifiers, and practical application.

Bless Nintendo for doing everything they can to make video games in an era of "cinematic experiences for mature gamers." They're not without failure, of course, and their past ventures into augmented reality are a good entry point for dissecting this matter.

The Virtual Boy was a head-mounted display (HMD) that used a parallax effect to create "true 3D graphics" in glorious red monochrome. Even Nintendo saw the folly of HMD and gave players a stand so they did not have to wear it on their face. Despite being brave, the platform never really took off and remained a niche device that only shows up in gags, adamant games enthusiast's collections, and the personal gallery of status-obsessed posers who want cred without knowing much of why they spent exorbitant amounts of money on something they don't use.

Practicality

The problem with the Virtual Boy is a problem all VR that use HMD run into: A disconnect from the rest of the world.

Sci-fi lied to us again with its foreboding messages of mankind eagerly forfeiting the real world for an empowering fantasy world of our own creation. That could never happen! People are too well trained to be consumers to produce things! Jokes aside, there is a severe disconnect with wearing an HMD and using a controller that we cannot see.

Between our tactile senses that remind us there's a couple pounds of plastic strapped to our head, and this phantom sense of a controller we feel but can't see, there's a great cognitive dissonance that prevents it from being a seamless experience. This doesn't even take into account that there will be sounds outside of the HMD we can't fully detect and necessary biological functions will require us to unplug to perform them.

Supporters of VR will tell you that it doesn't matter as long as the user really experiences "presence." Presence is essentially the VR buzzword analogous to "immersion" or "visceral" the mainstream games media likes to throw around now.

What "presence" means for VR is creating a satisfying, well-designed piece of software that encourages a great experience for the audience so much that they feel sucked into it. That's no small task and it's asking for trouble trying to dress up that concept with a single word.

The practicality of this kind of set-up is by far the biggest hurdle for any real developments of VR and I would be surprised if people widely adopted it.

Technology

Exposure to VR causes derealization and depersonalization—or, in other words, VR users can experience the feeling that the real world is not real or that their feelings and sense of self seem unreal. If you need more than the linked study a trip to the Oculus Rift forum shows that it's not just French Canadians but everyone experiences some altered sense of perception, which can be greater or worse depending on pre-existing factors such as anxiety or dissociative disorders.

Immersive VR needs perceived depth and 3D in games is usually gimmicky. Games are not typically designed around the user's ability to grasp depth of field as an important part of the gameplay.

The only time that 3D seems to have been well-implemented was with the 3DS, and I don't mean that it included a slider to turn it off. All the visuals on the top screen would display sort of like a diorama and the player could see the bottom screen and the rest of the world without stumbling over virtual disassociation. This effect worked perfectly for a game like *Super Mario 3D Land*, allowing the player to accurately sense the distance needed to jump. Unfortunately, this expert implementation of 3D is the minority.

Games

People aren't going to want what you're selling unless you have games or "killer apps" on it. Whether it be Virtual Reality, a game console, or even the new hot consumer electronic by the foreboding tech giant that wants to revolutionize how you interact with the world.

I'm talking about Google Glass. It failed.

The Nintendo 3DS has no shortage of good games but the 3D was an afterthought in most games design. VR takes effort to develop and while the media loves to write about how Virtual Reality is the future of games can you, the reader, name five or more games for the Oculus Rift that you're excited to get? How about ones that were actually made for it and not a port of an existing game like *Half-Life 2* or *Team Fortress 2*? How about five games for Valve's VR headset or Sony's PlayStation VR?

Google Glass exploded in popularity with that video of the hipster playing the ukulele on the rooftop and even more when celebrities and upper-crusty Silicon Valley types were seen wearing them.

It failed to take off not only because Google was slow to start selling the actual product but because it has no utility beyond being a Google App manager.

Remember how the media gushed endlessly about Google Glass?

Media

The lesson to be learned is that you have to be wary of taking the media at face value. Except for me and this article of course; because if you don't trust me (at least for now), we get into some weird Socrates Plato Liar Paradox. Take things with a grain of salt, in any case.

Solution

So what's the solution? Burn it all down and salt the earth? Do what I suggested at the start of this article and wait for someone who can think outside the box to get it right?

That might not be necessary. The solution may just be Augmented Reality. Google Glass was going in the right direction with lightweight headgear that is less obtrusive than standard VR

HMD but Google was too busy forcing Google+ on everyone to make it worthwhile.

You of course won't hear much about AR devices because that's not the sizzling hot technology that has had big money thrown into it, but it pops up here and there with various devices and at trade shows. Even the Nintendo 3DS had an AR functionality with the handheld's cameras and unique cards.

castAR may be the bridge between the VR and the real world that bides time until technology has sufficiently advanced to give us fuller VR simulation. castAR was invented by Jeri Ellsworth during her time at Valve but was able to break out into the future on her own after some tense experiences that deserve their own time.

It's hard to say if the castAR and similar Augmented Reality technology has what it takes to get a foothold against an adverse media, but if it wants to stand a chance it has to have games or something that will drive consumers to use it.

This is likely what Mark Zuckerberg was hoping for when he bought Oculus Rift after hapless Kickstarter backers had retroactively paid the billionaire's R&D bill. Training the consumer base to regularly use a VR peripheral is a good way to overcome preconceived notions, but let's be honest: Facebook isn't as popular as it used to be. At the very least it's "less cool" now and wearing a big dorky VR HMD when you want to see how great your ex's life supposedly is isn't going to combat the site's declining status.

I'll stick to regular video game simulation for now. I don't have the money to drop on speculative technology or know anyone status obsessed and ironically uncool that can get me some on the sly. Besides what good is a computer or console without worthwhile software?

> "We tried to convey or portray the
> emotional journeys of the victims
> through the events, which began
> at 8:46, and we wanted the appeal
> to reflect the feelings during the
> experience for many of the victims, of
> distress and desperation at the end."

Experiencing History Is Better Than Learning It

Luke O'Neil

In the following viewpoint, Luke O'Neil argues that though the virtual reality application that takes users inside the World Trade Center on September 11, 2001, is getting a lot of criticism, he is sympathetic to the developers' point of view. He finds that the application is not sensationalism. Instead, the application is meant to help users understand what happened that day. O'Neil is a journalist who writes for Esquire *magazine.*

As you read, consider the following questions:

1. According to O'Neil, why did the students develop a VR experience based on the events on September 11, 2001?
2. What has been some of the criticism of the 9/11 VR project?
3. Why do you think the VR experience was pulled from the Oculus Rift store?

"A Conversation with the Creators of the Controversial 9/11 Virtual Reality Experience," Luke O'Neil, *Esquire*, October 30, 2015. Reprinted by permission.

It goes without saying that the images of 9/11 are firmly lodged in our consciousness. But for those of us who weren't in New York at the time, when we remember that day, it's with the perspective of distance: images of the planes hitting the towers or billowing clouds of smoke rolling down the avenues. It was with that perspective in mind that a group of six students at the Cnam-Enjmin University in France approached the concept for their project "8:46," which they describe as a "narrative driven virtual reality experience." The premise of the project was to try to help the user "embody an office worker in the North Tower of the World Trade Center during the 9/11 events."

If *The Walk* reportedly made people sick in theaters, what will this do?

The game—although that's not exactly the right term for it—has been available in the Oculus Rift store for the past month, and the team, led by creative director Anthony Krafft and producer Pierre-Yves Revellin, told me over Skype that it has been downloaded for free about 4,000 times. That's a number that they expect to jump considerably since it recently caught the attention of the press. A lot of that attention, as you might imagine, has not exactly been welcoming. Fusion, for one, said that while there might be a use for a realistic 9/11 simulator, "this one feels a little gratuitous, especially for those of us old enough to remember the terror of the real, non-virtual September 11th." Elsewhere, online reactions have run the gamut from outright befuddlement, to woefully offended, to curiosity about what potential this might have as a teaching tool down the line.

Watching a handful of walkthroughs of the experience on YouTube, much of the criticism of the graphics and voice acting are more than fair. But then again, this is a student project. The moment of impact, itself, which is depicted in a surprise explosion, is scary enough, but the resulting smoke is pretty silly looking. Nonetheless, after talking with the team, it seems like this was less a sensational stunt and more the result of some curious students who were actually invested in their concept. Which isn't to say that sincerity is armor, but at least it's better than craven opportunism.

"9/11 was the turning point of our link to history for every one of us," Revellin said. "It has changed the history of our country and our society too. Quickly it began to be more than that, because we began to really dive into the subject, and we began to see the 9/11 attacks as something else than a televisual event or a history event, but also the personal, individual stories that constitute what is a historical event."

I wondered who, exactly, the target audience for a game like this even is.

"We never speak about *game*," he said. "We talk about it as an experience. It's not about fun, the goal is not to have fun, evidently. And so it's not a game."

Krafft said by using virtual reality, the team members thought they might be able to reach a larger audience in what they felt was an immersive way. "Virtual reality gives an experience, a sense of presence, which allows us to touch an audience much larger than traditional video games." They wanted to reach people who don't play games, he said. "We tried to target a mature audience, a curious audience, one who wanted to try new forms of art."

Whether or not you find it appealing art, or even competent art, will depend on your level of experience with VR—not to mention your thoughts on 9/11, itself, as it's often treated as a sacred cow that even the most conscientious artists are criticized for going near. But the end result, the team said, is supposed to make you feel something.

"We tried to convey or portray the emotional journeys of the victims through the events, which began at 8:46, and we wanted the appeal to reflect the feelings during the experience for many of the victims, of distress and desperation at the end," Revellin said. One of the interesting things they uncovered in their research, they said, was that for a lot of the victims, there wasn't necessarily a sense of urgency throughout the early stages of the attack, with some dismissing the danger based on the previous attack on the World Trade Center in 1993.

"We needed to put the viewer in the same place as the victims. It was a Tuesday like any other, a work day for us, but not for the victims."

While most of the team, whose ages range from 22 to 26, were very young when 9/11 happened, they all say they remember the day well. Everyone the team talked to who tried the simulation had a different reaction, they said, but that's part of the point.

"There has been some rejection, mostly from the premise of the project, even before trying the experience," Krafft said. "We don't have many people thinking we made an experience of sensationalism, which was very important to us. There are many floors in the experience, six people on the project, and it doesn't distract from the actual point of the experience. We have such varied reaction I can't tell you all. You can see today we have a lot of media attention forums with various feelings on the subject. It's very personal for each of the people."

In the middle of our conversation, the team got a notice that the product had been removed from the Oculus Rift store, perhaps owing to pushback from users who found it offensive. It was unclear to them at the time why it was taken down. Before too long it was back up again, they told me later.

"I think most of the time, people that think it is offensive didn't try it, and they think the principle of doing something about 9/11 is offensive in itself," Revellin, who has been to the Ground Zero site, said. "We can understand and accept this point of view, but we as artists can talk about what touches us. I think the honesty we tried to have, and the connection we had to the victim experiences by diving into every testimony we can have…we tried to do this with all the honesty and the care we are capable."

> *"The team has run many different experiments placing someone in the body of another, such as looking through the eyes of a migrant worker as they talk about their experiences, but the goal is always empathy, a connection with another person."*

Virtual Reality Helps Users Develop Empathy

Ben Kuchera

In the following viewpoint, Ben Kuchera describes virtual reality applications developed by BeAnotherLab that allow users to experience what it is like to be another gender. The purpose of the application is to develop feelings of empathy in the users. According to the author, friends and partners of dysphoric people can gain an understanding not easily achieved in other ways. Kuchera writes for Polygon, a gaming website in partnership with Vox Media.

As you read, consider the following questions:

1. What technology is required to allow participants to experience what it is like to be in the body of someone of another gender?
2. According to the author, what is the purpose of the gender-swapping experience?
3. According to the author, what are some challenges for applications such as the gender-swapping one?

It's disorienting to look in the mirror and see yourself as another gender.

I'm wearing my Oculus Rift development kit, and the virtual reality hardware gives me the illusion of being in a comfortable room in an Italian villa. There is a mirror in the room, and in it I don't see myself, but a woman. My brain doesn't quite know what to do with this information.

I move my head, and she moves her head. The illusion of being myself, but in the body of a woman instead of a man, makes me dizzy. I remove the helmet and put it away.

The demo *Girl Mirror Look* is a very rudimentary way for someone to experience inhabiting the body of a woman, but a group of artists, programmers, and activists are taking the idea much further by using low-cost virtual reality equipment to achieve something that sounds like science fiction: They're allowing people to trade bodies.

Becoming Someone Else

"How would you feel to swap your body with another?" Philipe Bertrand asked me. "Would you better understand the other if you see through their eyes?"

The cost of the equipment BeAnotherLab is using to create this illusion is modest: The group uses secondhand PlayStation Eye cameras, arduino-powered servos and motors to control the movement of the camera, laptops, and Oculus Rift headsets. Each set up costs around €500, or $685 but the "gender swap" setup requires two sets of equipment to function, one for each participant.

"In Brazil there are many problems with violence against women, which comes from their own partners," Bertrand explained. "What would it be like if a man could see through the eyes of a woman? Would he act in the same way?" The team has run many different experiments placing someone in the body of another, such as looking through the eyes of an migrant worker as they talk about their experiences, but the goal is always empathy, a connection with another person.

In the case of the more guided, narrative virtual reality experiences that don't require both subjects to mirror the movements of the other, the "performer" goes through different actions, while audio of them telling a story is played for the viewer. The viewer can look around freely using their virtual reality headset to explore the reality of the other person, the cameras are driven by motors and servos to give the viewer agency.

It may be hard for me to explain what it's like to get five kids ready for school, but imagine if you could watch the scene through my eyes, while I go about my morning routine, explaining everything to you step by step. You could look around to try to keep your eyes on the kids, or watch my hands as I clean bottles and make waffles. You'd get an actual sense of what my life is like, for better or worse.

Now imagine the same thing done by a factory worker in Foxconn.

These empathy experiments require a performer and a viewer, but the gender swap experiments require two parties of different genders to participate equally. Both parties, one man and one woman, wear the virtual reality headset and a camera.

The camera projects the point of view of the woman to the man's headset, and vice versa. The next step is something akin to calibration: you both reach out and shake the hand of someone in front of you at the same time. This allows your mind to lock into the other person's body. Not only are you seeing out of their eyes, but you're given the illusion of touching what they touch.

"This is the starting point of the embodiment sensation. People see themselves, you look around and see your body, look at your hands, they have the agency, and we shake hands usually," Bertrand explained. "It's stronger than touching objects, because it's the human touch, which is very strong. This is the connection that takes people into the embodiment experience."

This is an experiment you can do at home as well, and it's been used to create funny videos for talk shows. It's fairly easy to use the sense of touch to fool your brain into thinking it's inside an external limb or body, and you can then play with that sensation in interesting, or scary, ways.

In this situation one person begins to move their body in slow, deliberate ways, and the other person mirrors their movement. The idea is to flow together, to make it seem as if both parties are in control of their respective bodies. It's a sort of dance, where participation itself creates a layer of consent.

"Usually what happens is I start to do a movement, and the other is following me, and the other takes control of the movement, and I have to follow her. It's constant agreement," Bertrand said. "Like a relationship. You do a little bit for yourself, and a little bit for the other. It's very intuitive."

The illusion is effective, according to Bertrand. You don't feel like you're in virtual reality, you feel as if you're inside the body of someone of the opposite gender. "It's a beautiful thing," Bertrand said. "Gestures should be constantly agreed on by both users."

The sense of empathy can be powerful, and this leads to both parties being almost reverent about the body they're experimenting with. "People tend to be very respectful towards the other, and realize that the other body is from another person, and you don't invade this," he said.

This technology has many uses; there have been studies that show seeing yourself as someone of another race may decrease your implicit bias. One such paper showed you can use virtual reality to place someone in the body of a dark-skinned avatar, and the evidence suggests that this at least temporarily reduces implicit bias against that race.

"This effect appears to be specifically linked to racial bias since embodiment in an alien, purple skin virtual body towards which no stereotypes or prejudices can be automatically associated, did not result in the same response," the report stated. The implications here are fascinating: You don't even have to walk that virtual mile before you begin to empathize with someone of a different race.

There could also be healing value to some of the experiments, such as allowing someone in a wheelchair to "borrow" the body of a dancer to feel like they can move and dance again. Even if you can't walk or move again, if someone is willing to share their time and body with you, you can be given the illusion of doing just that.

"It promotes empathy between two people," Bertrand said. "At the end of the performance, the user tends to go to the performer and hug them and talk a bit, to try to understand more about their life. To create some kind of peaceful feeling of closeness and awareness of their social condition."

While Bertrand is quick to note he's not a scientist and has no background to discuss the potential mental health benefits of this technology, I did speak to at least one expert who thought the ability to explore the body of another gender could be helpful in treating individuals suffering from gender dysphoria.

Gender dysphoria is a state in which individuals identify as a different gender than their birth-assigned sex. My feeling of discomfort and unease at seeing a female form looking back at me from the mirror in the Oculus Rift demo gives one an indication of what it must feel like for someone who knows they are a man or a woman, but sees and feels the opposite reality in their body.

A Sense of Empathy for the Suffering of Others

Dr. Anne Vitale works in the field of gender dysphoria, and treats patients struggling with gender identity.

"I can see where this sort of virtual gender-role expression could be at least temporarily helpful," Dr. Vitale told Polygon.

Gender Stereotypes Persist in Virtual Worlds

A recent study completed at the Virtual Human Interaction Lab (VHIL) at Stanford University, published in the journal *Cyberpsychology, Behavior, and Social Networking*, tested this hypothesis by assigning 160 subjects avatars with genders opposite to their own and pitting them against variously gendered bots in math tests. They found that subjects performed significantly better if their avatar was male, competing against female avatars, regardless of their actual gender or math skills.

The VHIL researchers' findings suggest that participants with male avatars experience what the researchers call a "stereotype lift"—a performance boost caused by the awareness of competing against someone associated with a negative stereotype—when competing against female avatars in virtual reality. "This suggests that even when avatar-based gender representations are arbitrary, wearing a 'mask' representing a social category membership that is free of negative stereotyping (relative to a negatively stereotyped virtual identity) can be positively motivating," the researchers wrote.

In other words, sexist stereotypes about women don't dissipate at the threshold of the virtual—the VHIS report suggests that they continue on.

"How Gender Stereotypes Persist, Even in Virtual Worlds," Jordan Pearson, *Motherboard*, August 20, 2014.

"It is a form of cross-dressing in a way. The image you see on the outside is much closer to what you really want, than what cross-dressing would give."

Jessica Janiuk is a software developer who often speaks on gender issues and has blogged extensively about her life as a trans woman. "I know that video games throughout childhood growing up have always been a source of ... experimentation might work? Depending on the game, of course, because of course in many games you have male protagonists," she told Polygon.

"Back in college when *Second Life* was coming out, that was a great source of relief for feeling and seeing myself as the person that I was and I know there are many trans people who escape into video game land for similar reasons," she continued. "It allows them to be themselves, to create a character who represents how they see themselves."

Janiuk was excited to talk about the technology, and how it fit into her past uses of video games to explore gender. "Using virtual reality to explore that, and cope with your own feelings of gender dysphoria, I think, would be amazing," she said. "It's something that I've thought about since the Oculus Rift came out."

Other are a little more skeptical. Gaming journalist Sam Prell was assigned the male gender at birth, transitioned to live as female for 6 years, and is currently living as male again "There are a lot of expectations and harsh realities when you're going through gender dysphoria," he said. "If you're going through the physical transformation, there are a lot of things you have to either learn to accept, or that won't match up to what you expect."

The road to transitioning is long, and inhabiting a body you may never be able to achieve could worsen someone's self-doubt, he explained. "I would be cautious about using it, because I'm afraid it would set up unhealthy expectations," Prell said.

Dr. Vitale was also careful to point out the shortcomings of the technology. "The first issue I have is with tactility. As the male runs his hands over what appears to be a female body he will still feel male textured skin and hair," she explained. "He will also feel flatness even as he runs his hands over what appear to be 'his' rounded breast."

"The only way around this would be not to touch any part of the body," she continued.

Dr. Vitale was skeptical of how useful this technology could be to treat those with gender dysphoria, but she sees great value in allowing everyone to experience what it feels like to be inside the "wrong," body, or to experience a disconnect between how they feel and the body they were given.

"It should help cisgendered women partnered with gender dysphoric males to appreciate what gender dysphoria is and what drives their partner to seek relief through hormonal and surgical means," she explained. "The machine allows her to retain her female gender identity while seeing herself having a muscular hairy body, no breasts and penis and testicle appendages she might experience as being 'very wrong.'"

Prell echoed these thoughts. "You take a straight man and a straight woman who don't have any sort of gender dysphoria, and put them into this simulation, then I think you might see more beneficial results where you get more respect about intimacy and what's okay and what's not okay," he said. It's rare that you're able to give someone the feeling of being inside a body that doesn't match their gender, and doing so may help more people understand the challenges of transgender individuals.

Bertrand admits that the technology is new, and he's unequipped to deal with the possible medical or scientific value of the work the team is doing. They're looking for partners in the scientific or art world to help with taking the next steps, and of course funding is a part of that process.

The early results, however, have been encouraging. This is a new way for people to learn more about others, and themselves. "Using this system you can help people understand each other, and have more tolerance towards each other," Bertrand said.

"For those of us who live that feeling of dysphoria, we don't have that relief of being able to just lift the helmet off," Janiuk said. Experiences like the *Girl Mirror Look* demo prove that it's possible to give the rest of us a sensation of being in the body of the opposite gender, but this is only a taste of what people struggling with gender dysphoria are going through, and we can always remove the helmet. Even this limited understanding may be enough to help others feel more empathy, however, and that's a large achievement.

"I think a little bit of empathy," Janiuk said, "is something the entire human race needs more of."

> *"Virtual-reality simulations can help managers take tactical actions such as designing retail space that can entertain and persuade customers."*

Market Research Will Benefit from Virtual Reality

Raymond Burke

In the following viewpoint, Raymond Burke argues that using virtual reality is an efficient and cost-effective method to conduct market research. He claims that businesses can collect data on consumer brand loyalty, the effectiveness of product displays, and customer shopping behavior. He contends that using virtual reality applications increases the speed and lowers the cost of market research. Burke is the E.W. Kelley Professor of Business Administration at Indiana University.

As you read, consider the following questions:

1. According to Raymond Burke, what are the advantages of using virtual reality technology to conduct market research for product manufacturers?
2. How have marketing professionals used VR in market research?
3. What are the limitations to using VR for market research?

"Virtual Shopping: Breakthrough in Marketing Research," Raymond Burke, *Harvard Business Review*, Reprinted by permission.

M anagers know that in today's increasingly complex and competitive environment, they need to develop ideas that break through the clutter of messages in the mass media and the confusing array of products at the point of purchase. As Walt Disney once said, "You can't top pigs with pigs." Unfortunately, the more innovative the concept—whether it is a new product, package, price, promotion, or distribution plan—the greater the risk. Traditionally, companies have used marketing research to test shoppers' reactions to new ideas, thereby reducing risk. But although the past 20 years have seen a breathtaking rate of technological advancement on many fronts, most marketing-research techniques are, by and large, sadly outmoded. The tools most marketers employ are too expensive, vulnerable to observation and manipulation by competitors, contrived and unrealistic, or simply incapable of providing the information managers really need.

Technological advances in virtual reality offer new hope, opening opportunities in marketing research and beyond. Just as the vacuum tube turned radios into household fixtures and the microchip made personal computing possible, three-dimensional computer graphics have made simulated test-marketing practical for a broad range of companies and applications. Virtual-shopping simulation can help managers make tactical decisions in areas such as new products and promotions, packaging, and merchandising. Ultimately, the tool promises to change the way companies innovate and how they approach a variety of strategic issues that range from entering new markets to responding to a competitor's attack.

Current Practice

Before examining the virtual store more closely, it is useful to consider the research techniques most managers currently employ. Take the traditional test market. Let's say a company would like to test consumers' acceptance of a new product before rolling it out on a regional or national level. The company would produce a sample run of the product, and then the sales force would introduce it into a typical midsize market. Managers would use point-of-sale scanner data along with information on warehouse withdrawals and product shipments to keep track of sales and market share. This methodology has what marketers call *high external validity:* The product is sold in a natural, competitive context to a representative group of consumers. Unfortunately, the process is slow and expensive. One test often takes six months to a year or longer to complete and can cost millions of dollars. In fact, it usually takes 30 to 60 days just to get the new product onto store shelves. What's more, when competitors discover the test, they may try to disrupt it by increasing their own promotional activities, or they may copy the idea and rush their own new product to market. By the time the research has been completed, the market has often changed, so the results are uninformative.

A second approach is to conduct a controlled field experiment. A research company sets up distribution for the new product in a representative set of test stores while maintaining current conditions in a matched set of control stores. During the test period, the researchers handle inventory, stocking, pricing, and billing. Such a test is generally faster and less expensive than a traditional test-market initiative. But it has drawbacks as well. One is, of course, that the experiment is not as realistic as the traditional test market because the products are being handled differently— for example, the shelves are not being stocked by actual store employees. Another is retailer resistance. Retailers are reluctant to manipulate the selection and merchandising of their products in ways that might disturb their patrons. Furthermore, it is unlikely that one retailer will want to share the results of these studies with other retailers. And, as with traditional test markets, controlled store tests may alert competitors to a manufacturer's activities.

An additional problem with both tests is the high level of noise in retail sales data. Noise—unreliable variation in purchasing patterns—can make it difficult for researchers to determine the effects of specific marketing manipulations. For example, during one week in Jewel Food Stores in Chicago, Scott Paper Company's paper towels had a 47.7% share of the market; in another week, the same product had a 4.7% share. The fluctuation was largely a function of competitors' activities rather than of Scott's own promotions. Other sources of noise include out-of-stock conditions, manufacturers' advertising, and various political and economic changes.

A third marketing-research approach is to use questionnaires, surveys, or interviews to ask consumers what they like and dislike. Although there are several such methods for testing new concepts, the most common is the focus group. Groups of six to ten consumers are brought together at a research facility (often located in a shopping mall) to discuss their reactions to new products, packages, advertisements, or promotions. A professional moderator usually conducts the sessions, and the participants' comments are tape-recorded and transcribed for analysis. Focus groups are popular because the results are easy to interpret and the method is fast, inexpensive, flexible, and confidential.

Unfortunately, focus-group research has a number of severe limitations. The most frequently mentioned (but often ignored) problem is that the test results are not a reliable indicator of the reactions of the broader population. In addition, focus groups (and most other "laboratory" methods) lack realism on several fronts. The first has to do with the *marketing stimulus.* Consumers are often asked to react to written or verbal descriptions of concepts. They may also be given an artist's rendering of a product or a rough sketch of a product's promotional materials. However, in real life, consumers' acceptance depends heavily on how successfully the concept and the associated marketing program are executed. For example, whether a new fat-free frozen entrée is positioned (through its branding, packaging, promotions, and merchandising) as a diet product for weight watchers or as a meal for active, health-conscious adults can have a substantial impact on the potential market size and level of demand for the product. The second way in which focus groups lack realism is that they do not include the *competitive context,* even though most shoppers judge new products, packages, and promotions relative to existing offerings. As a consequence, this research method tends to underestimate the benefits of a truly unique marketing program. The third problem is that focus-group testing does not measure *consumer purchase behavior*. Focus groups typically ask customers to express their attitudes toward new products or services or to estimate their intentions to purchase the offerings. But although the resulting data can provide insights into consumers' preferences, they don't give managers the quantitative estimates of sales, market share, product cannibalization, and profitability that managers need to assess the company's options.

For years, marketers have searched for a way to re-create the retail store and track purchases in a controlled, confidential laboratory environment. Those initiatives have led to the development of a variety of simulated test-market (STM) services, including Assessor, Bases II, Designor, ESP, and Litmus. Although these services differ in the types of sampling, questionnaires, and modeling they employ, most share a common test procedure of exposing consumers to a new product or marketing program in a simulated shopping environment. In some methods, the manufacturer's product is shown along with competitive offerings in a photograph or slide presentation; in others, consumers shop from an actual shelf fixture stocked with products. In both cases, people who select the test product are given a free sample. They are asked to use the product at home and to report their intention to repurchase the product. Researchers then enter the trial and repeat-purchase rates—along with managers' estimated advertising and promotional expenses, distribution plans, and pricing—into a sophisticated analytic model that predicts sales volume and market share. Some STMs allow the client company to play what-if games with the model by entering different assumptions about the marketing plan and examining the impact on sales. Commercial services have reported impressive predictive ability, often within the range of 10% to 15% of actual sales volume.

Yet although the potential benefits of STMs are clear, their impact on marketing practice has been limited. In fact, a study by the Advertising Research Foundation found that more than

95% of the tests were conducted by consumer packaged-goods manufacturers. Almost all the tests were done on new products rather than on new packaging, pricing, or merchandising for established brands. Most companies used STMs late in the new-product-development cycle, and then only for those few products that they already had determined were likely to be successful.

The reasons for this limited use begin with cost. Research companies usually charge between $75,000 and $150,000 to test a single new product or marketing change. Although this may be a bargain when compared with the expense of a real test market, it puts STMs out of reach of all but the largest companies. The cost also makes it impractical to test a variety of different products, packages, merchandising or pricing strategies, or promotional programs. STMs also lack flexibility. Most require normative data to calibrate their forecasting models, to correct for biases in consumers' stated purchase intentions, and to provide category-specific benchmarks for successful performance. These data are often available for consumer packaged-goods products in well-established product categories but not for other products, such as durable goods or soft goods, or in service industries. Finally, because most STMs require the manufacturer to provide the finished product, packaging, and advertising for the test, they cannot be used in the early stages of marketing planning, when managers are exploring new ideas and such materials do not yet exist.

Virtual Shopping

Recent advances in computer graphics and three-dimensional modeling promise to bring simulated test marketing to a much broader range of companies, products, and applications. How? By allowing the marketer to re-create—quickly and inexpensively—the atmosphere of an actual retail store on a computer screen. For example, in the Harvard Business School's Marketing Simulation Lab, a consumer can view shelves stocked with any kind of product. The shopper can "pick up" a package from the shelf by touching its image on the monitor. In response, the product moves to the center of the screen, where the shopper can use a three-axis trackball to turn the package so that it can be examined from all sides. To "purchase" the product, the consumer touches an image of a shopping cart, and the product moves to the cart. Just as in a physical store, products pile up in the cart as the customer shops. During the shopping process, the computer unobtrusively records the amount of time the consumer spends shopping in each product category, the time the consumer spends examining each side of a package, the quantity of product the consumer purchases, and the order in which items are purchased.

Computer-simulated environments like this one offer a number of advantages over older research methods. First, unlike focus groups, concept tests, and other laboratory approaches, the virtual store duplicates the distracting clutter of an actual market. Consumers can shop in an environment with a realistic level of complexity and variety. Second, researchers can set up and alter the tests very quickly. Once images of the product are scanned into the computer, the researcher can make changes in the assortment of brands, product packaging, pricing, promotions, and shelf space within minutes. Data collection is also fast and error-free because the information generated by the purchase is automatically tabulated and stored by the computer. Third, production costs are low because displays are created electronically. Once the hardware and software are in place, the cost of a test is largely a function of the number of respondents, who generally are given a small incentive to participate. Fourth, the simulation has a high degree of flexibility. It can be used to test entirely new marketing concepts or to fine-tune existing programs. The simulation also makes it possible to eliminate much of the noise that exists in field experiments.

The most important benefit of the methodology, however, is the freedom it gives marketers to exercise their imagination. It transforms the simulated test market from a go-or-no-go hurdle that occurs late in the planning process to an efficient marketing laboratory for experimenting with new ideas. Product managers can test new concepts before incurring manufacturing or advertising costs, paying slotting allowances to the trade, alerting competitors, or knowing whether the new ideas are good, bad, terrible, or fantastic.

The Virtual Store in Practice

Different configurations of the virtual store have already helped several companies answer basic questions about their product lines and about consumers' behavior. The questions—and the companies' various approaches to answering them—provide a good overview of the technology's capabilities.

What is our brand equity in a new retail channel?

The Goodyear Tire & Rubber Company had traditionally sold its tires through its own retail stores but was planning to expand distribution to general merchandise outlets. In this new environment, consumers would easily be able to compare Goodyear's tires with competitors' on price, tread design, and warranty. Managers wondered how this change in distribution might affect consumers' preferences. What was the equity in the Goodyear brand name? Could Goodyear charge a premium price for its brand, or should it reduce prices or extend warranties to attract customers? What if competitors followed Goodyear's lead?

To address those issues, Goodyear conducted a study of nearly 1,000 people who had recently purchased or were planning to purchase passenger tires, high-performance tires, or light-truck tires. Each respondent took a trip through a number of different virtual tire stores stocked with a variety of brands and models. Across respondents and shopping trips, the computer varied the prices and warranty levels of the competing brands of tires. Goodyear's managers judged a tire to have strong brand equity if it could command a higher price than competitors' offerings, draw sales away from competitors when its price was reduced, and retain sales in the face of competitors' price cuts.

Goodyear found the results of the test valuable on several fronts. First, the research revealed the extent to which shoppers in different market segments valued the Goodyear brand name over competing brands. Second, the test suggested strategies for repricing the product line. Goodyear's managers found that by testing a wide range of prices, they could predict whether consumers would notice a given price change and how great a change was necessary to cause shoppers to switch brands. Finally, the data helped Goodyear to identify which of its competitors posed the greatest threats to its business and which competing brands were vulnerable to attack.

Do we offer a sufficient variety of products?

As part of an effort to improve profitability through category management, the senior managers of a major snack manufacturer sought to evaluate the efficiency of the company's extensive product line. To do so effectively, they knew that they would need a clear map of the category's structure; that is, they would have to identify the groups of products that consumers perceived as close substitutes for each other. If a company sells a number of items that fall in the same grouping, it may be able to cut some of the slower-selling items from the set to improve operational efficiency and reduce costs while maintaining customer loyalty and satisfaction. At the same time, it may have opportunities to launch new items in sets where there is little competition but large or growing demand.

This company competed primarily in one snack category. Yet in many retail environments, particularly convenience stores and vending machines, its products were sold alongside a variety of different snack foods, including cookies, cakes, crackers, chips, and candy. To learn about patterns of loyalty and substitution, the company created a virtual vending machine stocked with a broad selection of snack foods. Four hundred respondents, recruited from six shopping malls across the United States, purchased items from the vending machine on repeated occasions. In some instances, the respondents' preferred item was made "temporarily out of stock." That action allowed the company to measure the percentage of customers who switched between brands and between snack categories when a specific snack was not available. It also allowed the company to assess the demand for each kind of snack overall and by consumer segment.

The research revealed that consumers perceived the snack categories to be broader than the typical food-industry definitions, with consumers demonstrating a consistent preference for either sweet or salty snacks. Consumers' preferred snacks also differed markedly across age groups.

These results had important strategic implications. They suggested that the snack manufacturer was actually competing with a larger set of companies and products than its managers had initially believed. To maintain the loyalty of its consumer franchise and capture the largest share of its customers' snack purchases, the company would need to introduce several new products outside its original product line. In addition, managers would have to modify the company's strategy for communicating with consumers, its brand positioning, and its in-store merchandising and promotions to take into account the broader context in which consumers make decisions.

How should products be displayed?

When consumers enter the frozen-food section of a grocery store, they are greeted by long rows of freezer cases filled with packages. The selection of products is extensive, but the heavy glass doors, the chilling blasts of air when a door is opened, and the possibility that the packages will thaw all discourage shoppers from casual browsing. Given that situation, how should products be arranged so that customers can quickly sort through the clutter and find what they want? Is it better to group products together by brand (such as Stouffer's, Budget Gourmet, Banquet, or Swanson), by user (such as singles, children, or health-conscious consumers), by main ingredient (such as chicken or beef), by price ("value meals" or "gourmet meals"), or perhaps by some other criteria or a combination of these formats?

One major frozen-food manufacturer approached this decision by conducting a study that used multiple virtual freezer cases stocked with images of its own brands and those of its competitors. In one scenario, products were arranged to reflect the organization of packages in a typical store—horizontally by product form (such as individual dinners or family meals) and vertically by brand. In the second scenario, all the manufacturer's products were grouped together in one location, creating a billboard effect. In the third, most of the company's items were grouped together, but selected items were placed next to key competitors' products.

More than 400 respondents from five U.S. markets participated in the study, and the results revealed that shelf arrangement had a significant impact on sales and the time taken to reach a decision. However, the ideal organization depended on the type of product. For established products that had achieved high levels of brand recognition and loyalty, the billboard grouping made it easier for consumers to find the items and resulted in increased sales. For some of the company's newer products that were designed to appeal to particular lifestyle or usage segments, sales increased when the goods were positioned next to similar, competing products.

Before conducting the study, the frozen-food manufacturer would have faced the difficult task of trying to persuade retailers to rearrange their freezer cases so that some items would be grouped by brand and others by usage occasion, such as lunch or dinner, or by type of user. Few retailers would have wanted to tamper with a shelf arrangement that was familiar to customers and common in the grocery industry. Armed with its research data, however, the company was able to argue convincingly that a new format would make it easier for consumers to shop and also could increase both the manufacturer's brand sales and the retailers' category sales in the frozen-food section.

The issue of product presentation was investigated in a very different context by a chain of fast-food restaurants. Managers were worried that the company was losing lunchtime business because its customers were taking too long to order. Patrons would stand at the registers, staring at the menu boards and puzzling over the extensive and confusing array of alternatives. Others would walk away, frustrated by the long lines. To investigate the issue, the company designed multiple virtual menu boards with alternative groupings of items. Test subjects were then asked to place orders from the boards. The research revealed that grouping products together into meals with a small discount increased ordering speed and total order size for a significant percentage of customers, thereby increasing the total volume of business.

Companies were able to explore consumers' behavior in a confidential laboratory setting.
In each of the examples above, the unique features of virtual shopping allowed companies to address important issues that would have been difficult to study any other way. In Goodyear's brand equity study, the extensive *control* made possible by the simulation allowed the company to manipulate its products, prices, and warranty levels, as well as those of its competitors, systematically. In the snack substitution study, the *dynamic nature* of the simulation permitted the company to make changes in the available assortment of products based on the purchasing behavior of the consumers. In the shelf-display study, the simulation's *process-tracing measures*—its ability to track how customers shop, not just what they buy—helped the company to understand what effect changes in shelf organization had on consumers' attention and purchasing patterns. In all the cases, the companies were able to explore consumers' behavior in a confidential laboratory setting.

Integrating Virtual Shopping into Current Practice

Attempting to integrate any new technology into current company practice is not an easy task. Virtual-shopping technology is no exception. The following suggestions can help marketers minimize obstacles and maximize potential benefits:

Start small.

Build a computer-generated three-dimensional model of the smallest product category in which your company competes—including images of all the products in the category—and use it in a simple virtual-shopping experiment. The study must be easy for managers to understand and evaluate, and relevant to a current business decision. An excellent example is a pricing experiment. Pricing directly affects profitability, but managers often do not know what impact a price change will have on sales. Cross-brand price elasticities and consumer price sensitivity are difficult (and risky) to measure using field research but easy to study in a virtual store. Once the simulation data are collected, test the validity of the research results by taking an appropriate action in a representative market (for example, raise prices if price sensitivity and cross-brand price elasticities are low) and monitoring brand performance.

Benchmark the simulation against existing methodologies.

Most companies test new products with one or more in-house or commercial research methods, including concept tests, chip tests, conjoint analysis, and simulated test markets. The shopping simulation can be benchmarked against these methods by testing the same set of new product concepts with each approach and comparing the results. Differences in the time, cost, and findings of the research highlight the relative strengths and weaknesses of each method. The results can also be used to calibrate the simulation data for use with existing sales-forecasting models.

**Link the information systems of the people
who are creating, testing, and managing new
products and marketing programs.**

As noted earlier, two key benefits of virtual shopping are its high speed and low cost. For these benefits to be fully realized, a company must leverage its investment in information technology. In the packaged-goods and general-merchandise industries, companies use computerized systems to manage shelf space for successful merchandising and increased sales. The shelf-layout information, package dimensions, and product images from these systems can be used to construct three-dimensional models of existing product categories. New product concepts, displays, and promotions can be communicated electronically from the teams responsible for product design, research and development, packaging, and product management to the marketing-research staff. The images can then be used in the simulated shopping environment.

Develop standard measures of performance.
Computer simulations collect detailed information on what participants select across brands, product categories, shopping trips, and varied experimental conditions. As with UPC scanner data, simulation data can be overwhelming unless one chooses a small and meaningful set of performance indicators to measure the success of new marketing concepts. These measures might include the number of new customers attracted to the brand, the purchase rate of existing customers, the profits they generate, and the overall level of demand for the category.

**Coordinate the company's new-media
activities with marketing research.**
Each week, hundreds of new companies establish a presence on the Internet, offering a wide range of information, goods, and services. Most organizations see the medium as a new channel for communication and product distribution, but it also presents opportunities for doing real-time testing of marketing ideas. To facilitate research, the shopping interface should be designed to allow flexible presentation of information on the product. The interface should be capable of tracking customers and finding out how they search for and purchase an item.

Looking Ahead

Virtual-reality simulations can help managers to choose from a variety of tactical actions. These include reorganizing stores to make it easier for consumers to shop for the products and brands they want, designing retail space to entertain and persuade, testing the effects of advertising on consumer price sensitivity and loyalty, and managing categories (product assortments and shelf space, for example) to maximize profitability and store performance. These actions can be studied faster, less expensively, and with greater control and confidentiality in the virtual store than in the physical store.

Virtual-reality simulations can help managers take tactical actions such as designing retail space that can entertain and persuade customers.

But computer-simulation testing has other implications as well. For example, it can help managers decide whether and how to enter new markets. In many parts of the world, it is difficult to conduct conventional marketing research. In Mexico, for instance, consumer-panel data and UPC scanner data are of poor quality and have poor market coverage. Without a common benchmark, it is hard to know if an idea that was successful in one country could achieve equivalent results in another. With a simulation, it is possible to use a single, standardized methodology to evaluate the potential performance of new marketing programs throughout the world. One multinational company has begun to conduct virtual-shopping studies in North and South America, Europe, Asia, and Australia. Researchers create virtual stores for each country and region using the appropriate local products, shelf layouts, and currencies. Once the stores are on-line, a product concept can be quickly tested across locations. When the studies are completed, the results are communicated to headquarters electronically. The analysis reveals which markets offer the greatest opportunity for a successful launch.

Another critical element of business strategy is anticipating competitors' actions and developing marketing plans that are robust and contingent. Managers who make decisions under the assumption of a static marketplace do so at their own peril. With vigilant sales forces and sophisticated sales-tracking and exception-reporting systems, competitors are quick to notice and respond to a company's initiatives. One of the most common reasons for the failure of new products is unexpected retaliation by competitors. A marginally improved product may perform better than existing products under current conditions but may fail in the future if prices go down and competition intensifies. With virtual-simulation technology, companies can evaluate concepts under dynamic market conditions. They can test new ideas in virtual stores, trying out different competitive prices, promotions, and shelf allocations. The result will be solid marketing plans with consistently superior performance.

The virtual store has great flexibility. It can display an almost unlimited variety of products, styles, flavors, and sizes in response to the expressed needs and desires of consumers. Marketers can sit down with customers at the computer and collaborate on the design of new products and marketing programs. Merchandise can be shown in a variety of entertaining and informative contexts, including, perhaps, a model of the consumer's home. Home shopping is already a reality. One day, the virtual store may become a channel for direct, personal, and intelligent communication with the consumer, one that encompasses research, sales, and service. As one shopper summed it up, "This is what I read about in science fiction books when I was growing up. It's the thing of the future."

> *"Give it five or six years, and most computers will be capable of running good virtual experiences."*

To Become Mainstream Technology, Virtual Reality Must Overcome Challenges

Stuart Dredge

In the following viewpoint, Stuart Dredge argues that in order to become a mainstream technology, virtual reality must overcome three challenges. It must be compatible with smartphones, it must have applications in addition to games, and it must counteract negative physical reactions such as motion sickness. He contends that VR developers must consider the social benefits and costs. Dredge is a contributing editor to Guardian Technology.

As you read, consider the following questions:

1. According to Stuart Dredge, what are some challenges virtual reality technology must overcome before it becomes mainstream technology?
2. According to Dredge, what issues do the developers of VR applications need to address before VR can be used in filmmaking?
3. What do VR developers consider "the elephant in the room" when creating VR applications?

"Three Really Real Questions About the Future of Virtual Reality," Stuart Dredge, *The Guardian*, January 7, 2016. Reprinted by permission.

I s 2016 the year that virtual reality (VR) finally makes its breakthrough as a mainstream technology? That's a question for its evangelists and sceptics to argue about, and there are plenty in both camps.

With Facebook's Oculus Rift headset now available to pre-order, Sony's PlayStation VR and HTC's Vive on their way, and millions of cheap Google Cardboard headsets out in the wild already, this year will see a barrage of experimentation around VR.

Stepping back from the hype, there are three big questions—*really real* questions, you could say—about VR's potential, and as the answers emerge in 2016, we'll have a much better idea of whether this time round, the tech will be a hit or a flop.

How Mainstream Is this Technology *Really* Going to Be?

Facebook boss Mark Zuckerberg didn't spend $2bn buying Oculus VR to release a niche headset for high-end PC owners, even though that's pretty much what its first commercial version—retailing for $599 plus the price of a powerful PC (if needed)—will be.

"One day, we believe this kind of immersive, augmented reality will become a part of daily life for billions of people," wrote Zuckerberg in March 2014, when he announced the acquisition. Facebook sees VR as the next big computing platform, but that will depend on it becoming a truly mainstream device.

Oculus VR founder Palmer Luckey has acknowledged the challenge. "Most people don't have computers with high-end graphics cards. In the future, that's going to change: give it five or six years, and most computers will be capable of running good virtual experiences," he said at the Web Summit conference in December 2015.

"Right now it's going to be this niche just because of the equipment ... but you can still sell many millions of units."

He's right on the former claim. Chipset maker Nvidia predicted in December that in 2016, only 13m PCs will have the graphical welly to run virtual reality—less than 1% of the 1.43bn PCs in use globally this year.

VR isn't all about the PCs though. Sony has sold 35m PlayStation 4 consoles, and will be hoping to sell a few million PlayStation VR headsets to those gamers. But VR's path to the mainstream may be more about the devices we carry around in our pockets: smartphones.

Analyst firm SuperData has predicted that we'll spend $5.1bn on VR hardware and software in 2016, but that most of this will be on "cheap mobile VR devices" like Google Cardboard, the sub-$30 headset that smartphones slot in to.

Luckey isn't a fan, having recently described Google Cardboard as "muddy water" compared with the "fancy wine" of Oculus Rift, but that muddy water may be the current that takes VR to hundreds of millions of people in the coming years.

YouTube introduced 360-degree videos in March, and followed up in November with a format called VR video, for clips designed to be watched using a Google Cardboard headset, providing a sense of depth rather than just the ability to pan around. Facebook, too, is already showing 360-degree videos in the news feed within its Smartphone app.

Getting VR hardware into people's hands (or, rather, on to their faces) is the first barrier to the technology's success, but it's important to realise that it's as much about phones as it is about headsets and high-end PCs.

Will VR *Really* Be About More than Games?

When Oculus Rift first appeared as a $2.4m Kickstarter crowdfunding campaign in 2013, it was all about the games. "The first truly immersive virtual reality headset for video games."

When it ships this spring, it'll come with two games: Lucky's Tale and EVE: Valkyrie, with the promise of "more than 100 titles available by the end of 2016". Some of the world's top console, PC and mobile developers are working on VR games for the Rift and PlayStation VR.

And yet … VR will be about more than games. Zuckerberg was certainly thinking beyond gaming when he announced Facebook's Oculus acquisition.

"This is just the start. After games, we're going to make Oculus a platform for many other experiences," he wrote. "Imagine enjoying a court side seat at a game, studying in a classroom of students and teachers all over the world or consulting with a doctor face-to-face—just by putting on goggles in your home."

Already, several non-gaming uses are emerging to the fore: education and training; VR films; music and sports. Plus, inevitably, porn.

At the Web Summit, Luckey seemed particularly keen on education. "There's a lot of potential for virtual reality in the education industry," he said. "Classrooms are broken. Kids don't learn the best by reading books."

Perhaps not views that'll endear him to some teachers, but Luckey went on to suggest that VR could be a way to offer children virtual field-trips to places they wouldn't be able to visit in the real world.

"Even if visiting Paris for real is something that's better [than doing it with VR] it's not something that eight, nine, 10 billion people in the world are going to be able to do," said Luckey, Note, Google has already been trying to get schools to use its field-trip simulation software Expeditions with Google Cardboard headsets.

Some of the educational projects already unveiled—the British Museum's use of VR to transport visitors back to the bronze age; Irish startup VR Education's VR app based on the Apollo 11 moon landing; David Attenborough's work with a special VR exhibit at London's Natural History Museum; and NASA's PlayStation VR demo of how VR could help its operators practise using robotic arms on the International Space Station—are among the more convincing arguments for modern VR being about more than just games or gimmicks.

VR films—whether fiction or documentary—is another fascinating area for experimentation already, particularly on the journalism side

The New York Times' VR app has featured films about child refugees and candlelit vigils after the Paris attacks; producer RYOT's Welcome to Aleppo documentary focused on Syrian refugees, while another of its films focused on the aftermath of the Nepal earthquake; ABC News launched a VR film about North Korea's anniversary march; while "godmother of VR" Nonny de la Peña used VR to reconstruct the death of Trayvon Martin, a 17 year-old African American shot dead by neighbourhood watch volunteer George Zimmerman in 2012.

The film-maker Chris Milk has also made a series of documentary films pitching viewers into stories—a refugee camp in Jordan, Ebola survivors in Liberia, a massive protest march in New York—as if they were there. Many of these filmmakers and journalists see VR as a way to cut through viewers' complacency about disaster or war stories.

"Instead of sitting through 45 seconds on the news of someone walking around and explaining how terrible it is, you are actively becoming a participant in the story that you are viewing," RYOT's Christian Stephen told the Guardian.

On the fiction side, Oculus set up its own Story Studio division with a team of veterans from the film industry. It launched a short VR film called Lost in January 2015, and is working on Henry—"a heartwarming comedy about a loveable hedgehog".

Meanwhile, Lucasfilm has experimented with Google Cardboard and a series of short VR videos called Jakku Spy, released before Star Wars: The Force Awakens, while US startup Baobab Studios raised $6m in December to finish its first animated VR film Invasion!.

However, Pixar's co-founder Ed Catmull has cast doubt on VR's suitability for narrative fiction. "It's not storytelling. People have been trying to do [virtual reality] storytelling for 40 years. They haven't succeeded," he said in December 2015.

"We have a whole industry which is gigantic: games. Games is very successful. It's its own art form though, and it's not the same as a linear narrative. Linear narrative is an artfully directed telling of a story, where the lighting and the sound is all for a very clear purpose. You're not just wandering around in the world."

For some creatives, though, this is exactly the point: viewers will be able to explore the margins of their films, rather than simply follow the standard camera.

"If you're doing the job right, there will be layers of storytelling that can't be consumed in a single viewing. For example, there could be a foreshadowing of future events or events on the margins that could be just as thrilling or tense," film director Gil Kenan said in October 2015, welcoming the comparison to multi-layered Russian novels. "I'm trying to be the Tolstoy of the big screen!"

Can Our Bodies and Minds *Really* Cope with VR?

The third big challenge for virtual reality concerns what it does to us as humans—a question that's about more than motion sickness. Although that's an important part of it.

"The elephant in the room is disorientation and motion sickness," said Oculus VR chief executive, Brendan Iribe, in November 2014, albeit during an interview where he was claiming his company would crack the problem, while rivals may not.

"We're a little worried about some of the bigger companies putting out product that isn't quite ready," he said. "We're encouraging other companies, particularly the big consumer companies, to not put out a product until they've solved that problem."

Avoiding motion sickness remains a challenge. Witness the BBC reporter Zoe Kleinman's experience at the CES show this week, when she had to tear a headset off mid-demo for fear of throwing up—and this for a journalist who had been "quietly impressed" with VR, having tried several headsets before.

The Wall Street Journal recently laid out some of the health warnings that come with the current generation of VR technology:

"The experience can cause nausea, eyestrain and headaches. Headset makers don't recommend their devices for children. Samsung and Oculus urge adults to take at least 10-minute breaks every half-hour, and they warn against driving, riding a bike or operating machinery if the user feels odd after a session."

Such warnings are sensible, but could be a barrier to mainstream takeup of VR. But the bigger issues may be about what these virtual experiences do to our minds, rather than our bodies.

Milk has drawn attention to the fact that the "reality" part of VR may pose important questions for human beings.

"Think about how the technology scales, to the point where you're eventually incorporating other senses at further and further levels of fidelity," he said. "What you're talking about at some point is more than a medium, but is fundamentally an alternative level of human consciousness."

Milk was thoughtfully plotting out the potential of VR rather than scaremongering, but questions about the long-term effects of VR and the related augmented-reality (AR) field are being debated —even if sometimes those arguments (like the motion-sickness discussion) are being wielded against competitors.

The CEO of Google-funded AR firm Magic Leap criticised "stereoscopic 3D" headsets in February 2015, for example, suggesting that they "can cause a spectrum of temporary and/or permanent neurologic deficits."

"Our philosophy as a company (and my personal view) is to 'leave no footprints' in the brain. The brain is very neuroplastic— and there is no doubt that near-eye stereoscopic 3D systems have the potential to cause neurologic change," he said.

Stanford University's Prof Jeremy Bailenson has expressed similar caution about how VR may change humans.

"Am I terrified of the world where anyone can create really horrible experiences? Yes, it does worry me," he said in October. "I worry what happens when a violent video game feels like murder. And when pornography feels like sex. How does that change the way humans interact, function as a society?"

There's also the question of isolation, especially when VR involves shutting yourself off from the world around you by wearing a headset. When Oculus VR launched its Social Alpha app in October 2015, the promotional image seemed a rather chilling vision of how we might watch TV together in the future:

Too many of us already struggle to focus our attention on the friends and family we're physically with, because we're staring down at a smartphone or tablet screen. There's an argument—one that perhaps could be better addressed by VR evangelists—that virtual reality is a next level of physical isolation.

Some of them argue that it's the opposite, although the words chosen by Luckey in a recent Vanity Fair interview raised questions of their own: "There could be a world where VR replaces most real-world interactions," he said. "What will happen is for many low-value interactions, VR will replace a lot of those."

Some of those "low-value interactions" might be more important to us than we think. But that's why it's going to be important to talk a lot about the effect VR has on humans and our social interactions—for better and for worse.

There's plenty to discuss about virtual reality as a technology, but its future will be defined as much by its social benefits and costs.

Periodical and Internet Sources Bibliography

The following articles have been selected to supplement the diverse views presented in this chapter.

Erin Carson, "9 Industries Using Virtual Reality," *Tech Republic*, March 10, 2015.

Craysen Christopher, "Is VR Ready for Business Use? Six Industries Getting to Grips with Virtual Reality," *ComputerWorldUK*, June 10, 2016.

Issie Lapowsky, "Oculus' Founder on the Pros and Cons of VR for Social Good," *Wired,* April 23, 2015.

Lestyn Lloyd, "The Unique Challenges of Virtual Reality Development," *PC Tech Authority*, June 26, 2015.

Jon Martindale, "Virtual Reality Is Lonely, But It Doesn't Have to Be," *Digital Trends*, May 3, 2015.

Sharmistha Mandal, "Brief Introduction of Virtual Reality & Its Challenges," *International Journal of Scientific & Engineer Research,* Volume 4, Issue 4, April 2012.

Teresa Mastrangelo, "Virtual Reality Check: Are Our Networks Ready for VR" *Technically Speaking,* June 29, 2016.

Sarah E. Needleman, "Virtual Reality: Promising but Posing Challenges," *Wall Street Journal*, March 19, 2015.

Jeffrey M. O'Brien, "The Race to Make Virtual Reality an Actual (Business) Reality," *Fortune*, May 1, 2016.

Kevin O'Hannessian, "Virtual Reality Isn't (Just) Playing Games," *Fast Company*, July 27, 2015.

Amy Westervelt, "Could Virtual Reality Make Us Better People?" *Co.Exist.*, January 27, 2015.

CHAPTER 3

What Impact Will
Virtual Reality Have
on Human Behavior?

Chapter Preface

In a virtual world, a user becomes a superhero, using special powers to find and deliver insulin to a diabetic child just in time. When the user takes off his headset and returns to the physical world of a university psychology lab, he is the first to jump in and collect all the pens "accidently" knocked over by the VR experiment leader. The experience has made him more altruistic, more willing to help other people. In another experiment, users are shown more elderly versions of themselves using virtual reality technology. After the VR session, they decide to allocate more money to their retirement accounts. They have become more in tune with their older selves. Losing weight, quitting smoking, and exercising more are some of many healthy habits being modeled in virtual reality environments.

In experimental labs all over the world researchers are finding that virtual reality can have lasting impacts on human behavior in the physical world. For many experts, this is good news. In the hands of medical professionals and military instructors VR has the potential to instill life-saving behaviors in a risk-free environment. People can practice skills and react to emergency situations in simulated worlds until they feel ready to work in physical situations. The behaviors learned in VR environments carry over into physical ones.

Other researchers have huge concerns about the capability of virtual reality to change behavior. Advertisers and marketing experts have long known that media can impact people's decision-making activities. Television or smartphone ads subtly influence consumers to buy certain products. Product placement in movies and video games does the same. Advertising companies are beginning to talk about the expansive "real estate" in VR worlds and the number of "data points" that can be exploited to sell products. VR experts point out that it is no coincidence that the big technology companies interested in developing virtual reality for consumers make a great deal of their revenue selling ads.

Psychology and technology researchers have long studied the potential for video games to change behavior in negative ways. An American Psychological Association Task Force found that in 2014 90 percent of American children played video games and 85 percent of games contained violent content. Teachers, psychologists, and parents have seen firsthand or read reports about children becoming more aggressive after playing violent video games. Because of consumer demand, much of VR content being developed for the mass market is violent or has adult content. The depth of the immersion in VR experiences can have even more of an impact on users. Similar to video games, VR games may increase violent behavior or even cause psychological trauma, experts warn.

The potential for virtual reality to change behavior presents challenges to developers and users. VR is in early stages, and researchers admit that not much is known about its impact. Healthy people, experts suggest, will be able to distinguish between the real and the simulated. However, those suffering from instability, mental illness, or substance abuse might be more susceptible to manipulation in a VR world. The viewpoints in this chapter invite readers to consider the potential of virtual reality to change behavior in both positive and negative ways.

> "*Key to using virtual reality as therapy is the degree to which an individual identifies with the world.*"

Virtual Reality Has Therapeutic Applications

Bobbie Ticknor

In the following viewpoint, Bobbie Ticknor argues that virtual reality can shape human behavior for the better. The author uses research being conducted on sex offenders as an example of the benefits of VR as a therapeutic tool. If successful, the therapy will reduce crime and help society. Bobbie Ticknor is assistant professor in Criminal Justice at Valdosta State University. Her research interests include sex offender treatment and general correctional rehabilitation.

As you read, consider the following questions:

1. At what university is the research in question being conducted?
2. What behavioral disorders have psychologists treated with virtual reality therapy?
3. What factors does the author state as potential obstacles for using virtual reality in the treatment of sex offenders?

The quality of virtual reality systems—immersive, computer-generated worlds—has advanced dramatically in recent years, as can be seen by the expansive editorial from journalists testing Oculus Rift headsets.

University of Montreal researcher Massil Benbouriche has used this realism to help understand the impulses of sex offenders in order to find better ways of treating them. Key to using virtual reality as therapy is the degree to which an individual identifies with the world. Benbouriche uses a virtual reality headset and various audio-visual stimuli within a "cave," or a cube of screens, to provide an immersive experience to the participant.

Sufficiently Real

Virtual reality treatments depend on immersion and presence. Immersion refers to the level of awareness of the real world during a virtual session—fully immersive systems, such as the one built in Montreal, carefully control the environment and inundate the participant with all the necessary stimuli, minimising the need to interact with real-world objects in a way that would break the illusion.

If this is achieved, physical presence is established—when the virtual world is sufficiently convincing to be perceived as a functional representation of the real world. Self-presence is the psychological connection the participant feels to the avatar representing them within the virtual world. The greater the level of self-presence, the more likely it is that users will identify with their virtual representation. The degree to which individuals can achieve presence determines the likelihood that the things learned in the virtual world will transfer to real life.

In the University of Montreal study, the researchers recorded the participants' physiological responses to what they were seeing and hearing. They used headsets that track eye movements and record how long participants spent gazing at images. They also measured participants sexual arousal through penile plethsymography (PPG), which measures the flow of blood to the penis.

Combining PPG and virtual reality to gauge the behaviour of sexual offenders in the past has been criticised because of the possibility that they game the system by simply not looking at the images. The eye-tracking capability of the headset overcomes this problem, recording not just which computer-generated images of adults or children the participants view, but over which areas of the body their gaze lingers.

The differences in the data recorded when showing participants sexual and non-sexual, or nude and non-nude images, are compared. Studies have shown that the combination of these methods used in a virtual environment can effectively measure sexual interest.

Virtual Reality, Real Life Benefits

Virtual reality has been used in psychology as a treatment option for many behavioural disorders for more than a decade. Virtual reality therapy, together with psycho-therapeutic approaches such as cognitive behavioural therapy, has been used to treat disorders among the general population, as well as criminal behaviour.

For example, researchers in the US have used virtual reality to treat anxiety disorders, post-traumatic stress disorder, attention deficit hyperactivity disorder, and substance abuse. Recently, researchers at the University of Cincinnati used a virtual environment to deliver a 10-week cognitive behavioural-based therapy to improve social skills in a group of juvenile offenders. Using virtual environments has been shown to enhance rehabilitation by offering participants a safe, "no loss" environment during treatment.

Not a Tool for All Situations

There are potential obstacles to consider when using virtual environments to assess and treat sex offenders. The cost of the hardware and software development required to implement it is expensive. There's also the cost of training clinicians how to use it.

The very realism offered by virtual therapies can also throw up barriers. Potential side effects for participants include what is known as cybersickness, with various symptoms from eye strain, headache and nausea, to sweating, disorientation, and vertigo.

There are also legal and ethical considerations. In some countries, even computer-generated images of nude individuals, especially those of children, can be illegal. In any case, sex offender research suggests there are many risk factors underlying whether an offender will re-offend. Depending purely on the physiological responses recorded through virtual reality simulations may ignore these risk factors. Ultimately this could lead to false assessments of sex offenders, either that they are rehabilitated when they are not or vice versa.

It's a natural progression to use technology in the criminal justice system to help assess sex offenders and improve the treatments available; as technology has been used in other areas of criminal justice. It offers greater potential to customise treatments to each individual, uses the known beneficial effects of virtual reality-based cognitive behavioural therapy to boost offender rehabilitation, and can be used to gauge how effective a treatment has been.

With prison overcrowding and reducing budgets, this technology has the potential to improve lives and slow the revolving door in and out of the criminal justice system.

| "*As soon as a VR scenario engages emotions, presence is increased.*"

Virtual Reality Effectively Engages the Emotions

Julia Diemer, Georg W. Alpers, Henrik M. Peperkorn, Yousuf Shiban, and Andreas Muhlberger

In the following viewpoints, Julia Diemer, Georg W. Alpers, Henrik M. Peperkorn, Yousuf Shiban, and Andreas Muhlberger argue that there is a strong association between users' feelings of presence and their emotional reactions to a virtual reality experience. They found that for most VR scenarios, when emotions were engaged, users felt a greater sense of presence. They claim that if VR is to be effectively used in the field of mental health, researchers need to be able to determine how well VR can actually induce emotional reactions. Diemer, Shiban, and Mühlberger are associated with the University of Regensburg; Alpers with the University of Mannheim; and Peperkorn with the University of Wurzburg, all in Germany.

"The Impact of Perception and Presence on Emotional Reactions: A Review of Research in Virtual Reality," Julia Diemer, Georg W. Alpers, Henrik M. Peperkorn, Yousuf Shiban, and Andreas Muhlberger, *Frontiers in Psychology*, January 30, 2015. http://journal.frontiersin.org/article/10.3389/fpsyg.2015.00026/full.

As you read, consider the following questions:

1. According to the authors, what is the relationship between the emotional experiences of users and their perceptions of presence?

2. How are VR applications being used to treat specific phobias?

3. What conclusions do the authors draw from their research into the impact of presence on emotional reactions to VR?

Virtual reality (VR) has made its way into mainstream psychological research in the last two decades. This technology, with its unique ability to simulate complex, real situations and contexts, offers researchers unprecedented opportunities to investigate human behavior in well controlled designs in the laboratory. One important application of VR is the investigation of pathological processes in mental disorders, especially anxiety disorders. Research on the processes underlying threat perception, fear, and exposure therapy has shed light on more general aspects of the relation between perception and emotion. Being by its nature virtual, i.e., simulation of reality, VR strongly relies on the adequate selection of specific perceptual cues to activate emotions. Emotional experiences in turn are related to presence, another important concept in VR, which describes the user's sense of being in a VR environment. This paper summarizes current research into perception of fear cues, emotion, and presence, aiming at the identification of the most relevant aspects of emotional experience in VR and their mutual relations. A special focus lies on a series of recent experiments designed to test the relative contribution of perception and conceptual information on fear in VR. This strand of research capitalizes on the dissociation between perception (bottom–up input) and conceptual information (top-down input) that is possible in VR. Further, we review the factors that have so far been recognized to influence presence, with emotions (e.g., fear) being the most relevant in the context of clinical psychology. Recent research has highlighted the mutual influence of presence and fear in VR, but has also traced the limits of our current understanding of this relationship. In this paper, the crucial role of perception on eliciting emotional reactions is highlighted, and the role of arousal as a basic dimension of emotional experience is discussed. An interoceptive attribution model of presence is suggested as a first step toward an integrative framework for emotion research in VR. Gaps in the current literature and future directions are outlined.

Introduction

In virtual reality (VR), researchers can simulate intricate real-life situations and contexts to investigate complex human behaviors in highly controlled designs in a laboratory setting. These characteristics of VR have proven especially attractive for the investigation of pathological processes in mental disorders, and this technology has steadily gained momentum since the 1990s (Rothbaum, 2009). The main application of VR scenarios in this field is research into the processes underlying anxiety disorders and their treatment. Here, VR has become established as a medium for investigating threat perception, fear, and exposure treatment (Mühlberger et al., 2007; Rothbaum, 2009; Opris et al., 2012; Glotzbach-Schoon et al., 2013; Shiban et al., 2013; Diemer et al., 2014).

For research into emotional experiences and emotional behavior, such as fear, anxiety, and exposure effects, it is vital that VR can actually induce emotional reactions. By its very nature, VR as a medium is "unreal" and relies on perceptual stimulation (including perceptual feedback of one's own actions)—in particular, visual cues, sounds, and sometimes touch and smell—to trigger emotional reactions. Historically, the first VR scenarios applied in the field of mental disorders used powerful visual stimuli to provoke emotional responses, in particular, height (Hodges et al., 1995). Soon, more complex multimodal presentations of visual, acoustic, and vestibular stimuli were developed, for example, to simulate airplane travel (e.g., Mühlberger et al., 2001,

2003, 2006). Still, as it is the very nature of VR the emotional cues relied on perceptional simulations. However, more recent studies have highlighted the need to consider not only bottom-up processes of perception, but also top-down effects when it comes to understanding how VR can be emotionally engaging—e.g., a background narrative to a VR scenario may enhance emotional experience (Bouchard et al., 2008; Gorini et al., 2011; Mühlberger et al., 2012; Peperkorn and Mühlberger, 2013). What is interesting about this perspective is that VR, as a perceptual medium (e.g., all experiences may be interpreted as not-evidence based), enables researchers to dissociate perceptual, i.e., bottom-up input, and higher-level, i.e., top-down processes based on information, and to manipulate them independently to study their effects separately and in combination.

Another VR phenomenon linked to emotional experience is presence. Presence is a dimensional construct and describes the extent to which a user feels present in a VR environment (Slater and Wilbur, 1997; Schubert et al., 2001; Botella et al., 2009). Theories of presence can be divided into descriptive and structural models. Descriptive models focus on delineating the components of presence, like the model embedded in the Igroup Presence Questionnaire (Schubert et al., 2001). Via factor analysis, these authors identified three dimensions of presence: spatial presence, involvement, and realness (Schubert et al., 2001). On the other hand, structural models aim at an understanding of how the experience of presence is generated in the mind. These models focus on cognitive processes and generally suppose that directing attention to the VR environment (e.g., Witmer and Singer, 1998) and creating a mental representation of this environment (Sheridan, 1999) are necessary processes that enable us to experience presence (Sheridan, 1999; Schuemie et al., 2001). The most recent structural model of presence, proposed by Seth et al. (2012), goes beyond earlier theories. Their perspective is not limited to VR, but instead, Seth et al. (2012, p. 12) point out that presence is an everyday phenomenon, "a basic property of normal conscious experience." Seth et al. (2012) argue that extremes of disturbed presence (with regard to normal reality) can be observed, for example, in schizophrenia and depersonalization disorder. The basic precept of Seth et al.'s (2012) interoceptive predictive coding model is that presence rests on continuous prediction of emotional (interoceptive) states. For example, when expecting the encounter with an anxiety-related stimulus, the prediction would be fear, together with the changes the organism usually undergoes during fear. When encountering the feared stimulus, the organism compares the actual interoceptive state (fear and its symptoms) with the predicted state. According to Seth et al. (2012), there will practically always be a certain degree of mismatch. Seth et al. (2012) postulate that presence is the result of successful suppression of this mismatch between the predicted and the actual interoceptive state —i.e., the prediction prevails over the mismatch signals. The idea that suppression of information that is incompatible with the VR experience is vital for presence is not new (Schuemie et al., 2001). For example, Sheridan (1999) posits in his estimation theory that presence is the result of a continuously updated interior model of the environment, stressing the necessity for suspension of disbelief. However, Sheridan (1999) is concerned with the prediction of environmental, i.e., external events. What is unique to Seth et al. (2012) is their emphasis on the prediction of interoceptive states (rather than external events), which affords a crucial role to emotional experience.

The aim of this paper is twofold. First, we provide a review of current research into the relationship between perception and information on emotional experience in VR environments. Since exposure therapy has so far been the most common application of VR technology in clinical psychology, our focus lies on VR concerned with fear and anxiety in both healthy and clinical populations. We present a series of our own experiments that were designed to examine the significance of perception vs. conceptual information and presence for the experience of anxiety, and fear in VR environments. Second, an integration of the literature regarding immersion, presence, and emotional experience in VR is still outstanding. Different VR systems, diverging operationalizations of presence, and study samples ranging from healthy controls to patients with anxiety disorders make it difficult to draw firm conclusions. Based on a review of presence research, we suggest a new interoceptive attribution model of presence as a step toward an integrative framework for emotion research in VR.

Effects of Perception vs. Information on Fear

The most influential theoretical conceptualization of dysfunctional fear to date is offered by the emotional processing theory by Foa and Kozak (1986; McNally, 2007). According to this theory, dysfunctional fear can be viewed as a memory network comprising information about the feared stimulus (e.g., its characteristics), the fear response (i.e., behavioral plans concerning escape and avoidance), and propositions of meaning (e.g., association with danger or threat; Foa and Kozak, 1986). Importantly, this fear network can be partly or fully activated by input that matches part of the network. Fear, according to this theory, is an index of network activation and can be measured both subjectively and physiologically (Foa and Kozak, 1986).

Fear can be activated by at least two pathways: The perceptual (e.g., visual fear-related cues) and the conceptual (fear-related information) paths. Perceptual fear-related cues are assumed to rapidly evoke physiological and behavioral fear reactions, whereas fear-related information is expected to produce subjective fear reactions, but only a poorer physiological activation (Hofmann et al., 2008). Strack and Deutsch (2004) in their reflective-impulsive model of social behavior propose that impulsive, emotional reactions are fast, and governed by the laws of association (spreading activation), while reflective behavior is subject to more flexible, cognitive control. However, the impulsive and the reflective systems are supposed to interact, allowing conceptual information (input to the reflective system) to activate rapid emotional reactions (Strack and Deutsch, 2004). In practice the separation of the two paths is difficult to investigate as emotionally relevant situations typically comprise input to both paths simultaneously.

Virtual reality is a particularly suitable tool as it offers an opportunity to differentiate the two paths for eliciting emotion. In VR, cue propositions can be activated by presenting feared objects perceptually (e.g., visually), and, unrelated to the perceptual presentation, activating the meaning propositions by informing a person of the existence of a feared object, or situation outside the VR scenario they are immersed in. The laboratory setting of VR further allows the online assessment of different fear reactions (subjective, physiological, and behavioral) in a highly controlled setting.

Empirical Findings on Specific Phobia

In a series of studies we investigated the relative importance of perceptual fear-related cues and conceptual fear-related information on the activation of fear in different anxiety disorders. We assumed that fear reactions in specific phobia (animal type) are primarily caused by simple perceptual fear-related cues like a spider, whereas the impact of information on fear (i.e., knowing about the presence of a spider without seeing it) should be less pronounced. We directly and separately manipulated the two paths by using VR to present the visual cues on the one hand and the independent information about the existence of a real fear-evoking stimulus on the other hand.

In a first study with patients suffering from spider phobia (Peperkorn et al., 2014), we found that specific perceptual cues (in this case visual simulations of a spider) and conceptual information (verbal report that an unseen spider was present in front of the participant) presented separately activated the fear network, albeit via different routes. Specifically, perceptual cues vs. conceptual information led to different degrees of fear activation, with the perceptual route being significantly more fear provoking than the informational route, as was expected for spider phobia. Fear ratings (mean of five exposure trials) of this experiment are shown in Figure 1.

In a second study, we addressed the question whether these findings generalize to other types of phobias. While in spider phobia, fear is characteristically triggered by a stereotypical object (the animal), in other phobias—those of the situational subtype, e.g., claustrophobia—triggers are more context-related, involving more complex perceptual stimuli (American Psychiatric Association, 2013). Therefore, we used the same design in a sample of patients suffering from claustrophobia (Shiban et al., submitted). Similar to the spider phobia study (Peperkorn et al., 2014), we found for claustrophobia that the perceptual condition (seeing the inside of a virtual box with a closed door) initially activates stronger self-reported and physiological fear responses compared to the information condition where patients knew they sat in an actual, closed claustrophobic box (the fear-specific information), but saw an open door in the corresponding VR environment. It is important to note that although both studies used mainly visual cues as perceptual cues, in the spider phobia study the cues were specific (a virtual spider), whereas in the claustrophobia study they were more complex and context-related (a claustrophobic box).

In summary, in these studies we demonstrated for the first time in an integrated multimodal experiment that perceptual cues and conceptual information can provoke fear reactions in specific phobia, with additive effects if combined. Interestingly, perceptual cues alone seem to induce more self-reported fear than information alone, regardless of the type of specific phobia (animal vs. situational subtype). This is in line with findings that fear enhances perceptual, but not mental processing (e.g., Borst and Kosslyn, 2010), implying that there is a closer link between perceptual input and the experience of fear, than between fear and the mental processing of (purely conceptual) information.

Empirical Findings for Social Anxiety

As social fears are generally thought to be more cognitive in nature than specific phobias (Clark, 2005; Schulz et al., 2008; Wieser et al., 2010), we expected—in contrast to the results from studies on specific phobia—that anticipating a speech would be more fear-provoking when conducted in front of an audience a participant is informed are there (even if not seeing the audience: information condition) than in front of a virtual audience (perceptual cues) when knowing that actually no one will listen to the talk. Therefore, in a third study we applied a modified version of the paradigm described above to a public speaking challenge (Shiban et al., 2014; Diemer et al., in preparation). In contrast to the studies of specific phobia, anticipatory anxiety was chosen to avoid a possible confound in the physiological variables due to arousal caused by speaking (Gramann and Schandry, 2009). Also, anticipatory anxiety has been shown to share important parts of the neural network of acute anxiety (Nitschke et al., 2006).

We hypothesized that a real observer outside VR (information condition) would evoke significantly stronger subjective and physiological fear reactions than a visual observer in VR (perceptual cue condition). Further, we expected that a combination of real and VR audience (combined condition) would result in the strongest subjective and physiological fear reactions. The experimental conditions are presented in Figure 2. Finally, we expected high socially anxious participants to show stronger fear reactions than low socially anxious participants. We randomly allocated 48 healthy participants to either the information condition, the cue condition, or the combined condition. (for details of physiological data acquisition, see Peperkorn et al., 2014). As expected, socially anxious participants reported significantly higher subjective fear, but there were no differences between conditions (see Figure 3). Physiological parameters [heart rate, skin conductance level (SCL)] decreased significantly over time. There was a trend SCL to differ between groups, with the highest SCL in the visual cue condition ($p = 0.066$), but there were no other effects of social anxiety or condition. With a mean Social Phobia Inventory (SPIN; Connor et al., 2000) score of 21.8 (median: 21, SD: 10.5), our sample was above the mean of healthy controls (M = 12.1, SD = 9.3), but markedly below the mean (M = 41.1, SD = 10.2) of patients with social phobia reported by Connor et al. (2000). While these results are disappointing in sofar as we could not find the expected effect of the information condition, the paradigm has shown promise. There was a clear effect of social anxiety, with significantly higher subjective fear in socially anxious participants, and in contrast to the studies on specific phobia, no superiority of the cue condition was found (Shiban et al., 2014; Diemer et al., in preparation). Therefore, we believe that it would be worthwhile to apply this paradigm in a larger sample of patients with social anxiety disorder, and to assess acute fear during public speaking.

Summary

In summary, the VR designs reported here confirmed the possibility of eliciting fear reactions via different routes (perceptual vs. conceptual). Patients with specific phobia seem to be particularly sensitive to perceptual cues. Interestingly, this finding was the same for spider phobia (animal type) and claustrophobia (situation type). For social anxiety, no differences in activation of the fear structure between the two paths were found. These observations are in line with Foa and Kozak's (1986) prediction about differential sensitivities of different anxiety disorders to different media of exposure (in vivo cues vs. imagination). However, the interpretation of our results on social anxiety remains preliminary, as we did not assess patients or acute fear as in the studies of specific phobia. It seems worthwhile to continue this research with different kinds of specific phobias and more complex anxiety disorders like agoraphobia, panic disorder, and social anxiety disorder.

Presence and Emotion in VR

The association of presence and emotional experience in VR exposure therapy is an issue of debate. Presence is commonly regarded as a necessary mediator that allows real emotions to be activated by a virtual environment (Parsons and Rizzo, 2008; Price et al., 2011). While this conception implies a causal role for presence, research has not yet been able to clarify the relationship between presence and emotional experience in VR.

Presence has been conceptualized, and consequently operationalized and manipulated, in very different ways. These range from a manipulation of presence by providing more or less sophisticated VR technology to the diverse methods of assessing presence, either by subjective ratings taken online during the VR experience, or afterward via questionnaires. Presence questionnaires vary greatly with regard to the constructs they measure; however, what they have in common is that they ask participants for a subjective judgment regarding their experience of presence. With this in mind, we will use the definition of Slater and Wilbur (1997) and Slater (1999) and call any manipulation at the level of technology a manipulation of immersion, rather than presence. Presence is defined as a subjective phenomenon that results from experiences induced by immersive VR technology (Slater and Wilbur, 1997; Slater, 1999; Schubert et al., 2001). To avoid confusion with aspects of immersion (technology), for the purpose of this paper, only subjective measures of the presence experience (ratings or questionnaires) are considered presence measures. We chose not to include physiological parameters as indicators of presence as physiology is directly linked to emotional arousal, so considering physiological responses as operationalizations of presence would inevitably bring a confound of presence and emotion. The following section on presence and emotion considers two approaches to presence. First, the effects of immersive VR technology on presence and emotion are considered. Then, we will take a closer look at correlative findings of presence and emotion.

The Role of Immersion

Immersion and presence

VR simulations can be more or less graphically enhanced, multimodally integrated, and interactive. More sophisticated technology is often thought to result in more presence. Already Botella et al. (1999) reported more emotional reactions to a simple, neutral VR scene when a high-quality head-mounted display (HMD) was used, compared to a medium-quality HMD. Typically, studies assessing different degrees of immersion find higher presence in more immersive VR systems compared to less sophisticated setups. Such effects have been reported for VR scenarios presented via a Cave Automatic Virtual Environment (CAVE) vs. HMD (Krijn et al., 2004; Juan and Perez, 2009), for HMD vs. computer monitor (Gorini et al., 2011), video wall (a large stereoscopic projection screen) vs. computer monitor (Baños et al., 2004), for active vs. passive navigation in VR (Freeman et al., 2005), and for stereoscopy vs. monoscopy (Ijsselsteijn et al., 2001; Ling et al., 2012). Although some researchers have failed to find an effect of immersion on presence (e.g., Baños et al., 2008, for stereoscopy), in general, research indicates that more sophisticated simulations (higher immersion) result in increased presence, especially in virtual environments not designed to induce particular emotions (Baños et al., 2004).

Immersion and emotion

As for possible effects of immersion on emotions, the picture becomes more complicated. While some authors report an increase in emotional responses in more immersive compared to less immersive VR systems (Botella et al., 1999; Juan and Perez, 2009; Visch et al., 2010), others did not find effects of immersion on emotion (Freeman et al., 2005; Ling et al., 2012). In more detail, it seems that immersion effects on emotion might depend on the nature of the emotions under study. Visch et al. (2010) suggest that the effect of immersive technology is mediated by arousal.

This idea appears plausible, as especially fear and anxiety, both of which are strongly arousing emotions, have been found to be stronger in more immersive VR setups (Juan and Perez, 2009), while happiness and relaxation appear to be much less influenced by the technology used (Freeman et al., 2005; Baños et al., 2008). Of note, the positive emotions induced in the studies by Freeman et al. (2005) and Baños et al. (2008) were not only of different valence than fear, but also non-arousing in nature. In a study of spider phobia, we also found stronger subjective and behavioral (avoidance) fear reactions in a stereoscopic vs. monoscopic VR (Peperkorn et al., submitted). By contrast, Ling et al. (2012) did not find an effect of stereoscopy on emotional reactions including fear. However, Ling et al. (2012) investigated healthy participants during a speech task, so arousal levels (mean heart rate about 75 beats per minute) appear to have been comparatively low.

Another possibility to test the influence of immersion is the use of different perceptual modalities or multimodal perceptual cues. Thus, we compared tactile cues (touching a spider model) with visual cues (visual VR spiders presented in the HMD) in patients with spider phobia (Peperkorn and Mühlberger, 2013). As expected, the combination of visual and tactile cues led to the highest fear ratings. Tactile cues alone activated significantly stronger fear reactions than visual cues alone. Interestingly, presence was also higher in the multimodal (perceptual plus tactile cues) than the single modus conditions, a finding that confirms the association of immersion and presence. However, the different perceptual paths that we investigated are few out of many; for example, acoustic stimuli can be important in specific phobia, and can be easily implemented in VR (Taffou et al., 2012).

Taken together, there is considerable evidence that the level of immersion a VR system provides exerts an effect on the presence experienced by the user (Ijsselsteijn et al., 2001; Freeman et al., 2005). This effect seems to be particularly prominent in the absence of emotional manipulations, i.e., the effect does not seem to be mediated by emotion. The fact that immersion does not per se increase emotional experience, but that the emotionally enhancing effect of immersion might be limited to arousing emotions (see the discussion above), supports this conclusion. For example, Baños et al. (2004) independently manipulated immersion (HMD vs. computer monitor vs. video wall) and emotional content (sad vs. neutral) of a VR scenario. They found an interaction effect, with immersion affecting presence ratings in the emotionally neutral condition, but much less so in the emotional (sad) condition. There was also a main effect of emotion, with higher presence in the emotional than in the neutral condition (Baños et al., 2004). However, it is not clear from these data why there was no immersion effect on presence in the emotional condition; unfortunately, Baños et al. (2004) do not report the strength of the actual emotions experienced by their participants. As manipulations of immersion are not direct manipulations of presence, it is impossible to determine from these findings whether presence is causal for emotional experience. It has been argued that immersion causes arousal, which in turn increases presence and emotion ratings (Visch et al., 2010). We will come back to the issue of arousal in the following section on correlative findings.

Presence and Emotion

The association of presence and emotion has been mainly investigated by means of correlations between these two measures. Correlations between presence and emotional experience in VR have been consistently reported, especially in the literature on VR exposure therapy (Robillard et al., 2003; Price and Anderson, 2007; Riva et al., 2007; Bouchard et al., 2008; Alsina-Jurnet et al., 2011; Price et al., 2011), although some researchers have reported no relation between presence and the extent of experienced fear (Krijn et al., 2004). A common conclusion in this type of research is that in VR exposure therapy, presence and fear appear mutually dependent (Robillard et al., 2003; Price and Anderson, 2007). In a recent study, we confirmed the positive association, but additionally found indications that the relationship between presence and fear might change dynamically during exposure to phobic stimuli (Peperkorn et al., submitted). Interestingly, a general effect of presence on treatment outcome could not be established (Krijn et al., 2004; Price and Anderson, 2007), although Price et al. (2011) found that scores on the presence subscale "involvement," but not other presence scales, predicted treatment outcome in a sample of patients with social phobia (n = 31) undergoing VR exposure therapy.

In the case of fear in non-patients, results are less clear. On the one hand, there are results paralleling findings from patient samples. For example, Alsina-Jurnet et al. (2011) exposed a large sample (n = 210) of test-anxious students and non-anxious students (groups assigned according to questionnaire scores) to a VR environment that simulated a university exam, and a neutral VR. The authors reported no correlation between fear and presence in the neutral VR, and a considerably stronger correlation between presence and fear in the test anxious group (Alsina-Jurnet et al., 2011). We found similar results in a sample of spider fearful and control participants exposed to VR spiders, with significantly stronger presence in the fearful participants vs. controls, and a significant positive correlation between presence and fear in the fearful participants only (Peperkorn and Mühlberger, 2013). Whether this pattern of results is related to a floor effect and/or reduced variability in fear ratings in the healthy samples has not been investigated. On the other hand, research on emotions other than fear tends to produce mixed results. In an emotion induction paradigm in VR, Baños et al. (2004, 2008, 2012) tested the effects of different kinds of emotion on presence. They found correlations between presence and emotion in healthy controls for sadness (Baños et al., 2004), joy (Baños et al., 2008), and relaxation (Baños et al., 2008). Using non-immersive VR equipment, Baños et al. (2012) could not find significant correlations between emotion (joy, relaxation) and presence; however, they did observe relatively high presence ratings. By contrast, using a relaxation paradigm presented with different levels of immersion, Freeman et al. (2005)

found only one significant correlation between the experience of happiness and a presence scale, which the authors interpreted as an artifact due to item overlap.

Interestingly, some authors have also tested the effects of emotions induced by information on presence. Gorini et al. (2011) had participants search for a blood container in a VR hospital, either with the information that this was urgently needed to save a child, or without this information. Bouchard et al. (2008) informed patients with snake phobia that there were snakes in a VR environment, while in fact, no snakes were shown. Both Bouchard et al. (2008) and Gorini et al. (2011) reported that this emotionally relevant background information enhanced presence, indicating a causal influence of emotions on presence. Other possible influences on presence could be personality or (spatial) intelligence (Alsina-Jurnet and Gutierrez-Maldonado, 2010). However, little is yet known about the influence of these, or other, traits on presence or emotion during a VR experience.

Taken together, results show that the stronger the feelings involved, either because of the nature of the emotion (e.g., fear vs. joy vs. relaxation), or because of the nature of the sample (patients with anxiety disorder vs. normal controls), the greater the likelihood of finding a significant correlation between presence and emotion. A possible explanation for this phenomenon could again be arousal. Already, Freeman et al. (2005) suggested that the correlation of presence and emotion might be limited to arousing stimuli. They proposed an arousal theory of presence, arguing that arousal leads to alertness, which in turn leads to higher presence ratings. According to Freeman et al. (2005, p. 2018), alertness increases a participant's readiness to respond to the stimuli that compose a given VR, as arousal represents a "call to action" – thus leading to a greater perceived physical and mental presence in VR. So far, this arousal theory has not been rigorously tested, although objective measures of arousal (i.e., physiological parameters) can be easily assessed during VR sessions (Mühlberger et al., 2007; Diemer et al., 2014). First evidence for a crucial role of arousal comes from the study by Gorini et al. (2011), who reported significantly higher heart rate in the group that experienced the hospital VR with a narrative that increased the relevance of the scenario. Unfortunately, Gorini et al. (2011) do not report correlations between heart rate and presence ratings.

Discussion

The findings reviewed here highlight important advances in the study of fear and anxiety in VR environments. The data on perceptual fear cues and conceptual information show that both are viable triggers of fear reactions (Bouchard et al., 2008; Gorini et al., 2011; Peperkorn et al., 2014; Shiban et al., in preparation). There is evidence that patients with specific phobia react more strongly to visual cues than to fear-specific information, a finding that lends preliminary support to dual-process theories like the impulsive–reflective model of social behavior (Strack and Deutsch, 2004). The possibility of activating fear separately by perceptual cue or information in VR opens up new research opportunities to investigate pathological processes specific to each route. This might be particularly relevant for cue-independent fears and anxiety, for example in obsessive–compulsive disorder, illness anxiety disorder, and generalized anxiety disorder.

As for presence, the literature shows the significance of immersion on presence. Specifically, greater immersion of a VR system increases presence, particularly in emotionally neutral VR scenarios, which indicates that the effect is not mediated by emotion. In fact, it seems that the "depth" of a VR experience in terms of presence and emotion is more strongly influenced by factors quite apart from the technological quality of the VR system. Certainly the effect of immersion – i.e., technological quality – on presence exists, but interestingly, it is strongest when no emotion is involved. As soon as a VR scenario engages emotions, presence is increased. Studies that manipulate emotion independently of the technological aspects and even the stimuli presented via VR (e.g., Gorini et al., 2011) demonstrate this effect quite convincingly.

Further, correlations between (strong) emotions and presence have been consistently reported. The effects of immersion and emotion on presence are possibly explained by arousal (Freeman et al., 2005; Visch et al., 2010), but theories of emotion and presence in VR (Freeman et al., 2005; Seth et al., 2012) have so far been insufficiently tested. In the case of VR exposure therapy, neither general presence nor immersion seem to be related to treatment outcome (Mühlberger et al., 2005); rather, a certain degree of both appears a necessary requirement for VR exposure therapy, but increasing either does not per se enhance therapy effects (Krijn et al., 2004; Price and Anderson, 2007).

Before the findings reported here can be integrated into one model, more research is needed. While the data resumed so far indicate a crucial role for arousal, the position of arousal in an explanatory framework that comprises VR system factors, immersion, aspects of stimulation (e.g., perception vs. information), presence and emotion is not clear. First, we do not know how the effect of perception vs. information on emotion is produced. On the one hand, fear-related elements in VR are input cues to the fear network—as proposed in emotional processing theory (Foa and Kozak, 1986)—and might thus directly enhance emotional arousal. However, this theory does not explain why, in specific phobia, perceptual cues have a stronger effect on fear network activation than information alone. The reflective–impulsive model of social behavior (Strack and Deutsch, 2004) can explain different effects of perception vs. information on fear. On the other hand, however, emotionally relevant perceptual stimuli and information enhance a VR environment, making it more interesting, appealing to attention and ultimately, increasing, at least initially, arousal—irrespective of the emotional valence of the stimuli in question. Since arousal is a basic dimension of emotional experience, the effect of perception and information on emotion might be mediated by arousal. The role of arousal should be tested with emotions with different levels of arousal, using in particular physiological indicators of arousal. To broaden the range of emotions investigated, anger would be interesting as a highly arousing emotion other than fear that could also be activated in VR.

Concerning presence, the preliminary conclusion we would draw from the findings reviewed here is that the case for a crucial involvement of arousal in the experience of presence is compelling. However, the mechanism of this effect cannot be discerned yet. Freeman et al. (2005) propose that arousal increases presence by enhancing attention to a VR environment and the possibilities of action offered by this environment. A different explanation we suggest is an interoceptive attribution model of presence.

Since presence is a subjective experience, common measures of presence explicitly call the participants to make a judgment of the degree of presence they feel in VR. Based on the results reviewed in this paper, we propose that participants make this judgment based mainly on two sources of information: (1) immersion and (2) the degree of arousal they feel. As for immersion, participants might base their presence judgment on the perceptual distance they experience from the real world setting, i.e., the less stimulation they receive from the real world, and the more stimulation from the VR scenario, the higher the level of presence they will indicate. Of course, this hypothesis needs further empirical confirmation. With regard to emotion, we believe that participants will give higher presence ratings if they feel emotionally affected. As arousal is a particularly strong indicator of emotional involvement, arousing emotions should lead to higher presence ratings, and correlate more closely, with presence ratings, than calm or serene emotional states—a picture that is in fact found in the literature. Interestingly, whether the experience of arousal per se, or the attribution of this arousal to the VR scenario is necessary for the experience of presence has not yet been investigated. Additionally, immersion itself is likely to increase arousal (Visch et al., 2010). In essence, the cognitive nature of presence—in that it is a subjective judgment—forms the core of our understanding of presence as it is usually conceptualized and assessed in its relation to immersion, stimulation, and emotion in VR research. We believe that our model is compatible with the predictive coding mechanisms put forward by Seth et al. (2012). In contrast to Seth et al.'s (2012) conception, our model focuses on the attribution process that gives rise to cognitive presence judgments. It is intended as a framework for research into emotional experience and presence in VR. Future studies should therefore differentiate as precisely as possible between cognitive presence (presence as a subjective judgment), emotional presence (Seth et al., 2012), and on the other hand immersion (technological features of a given VR system), arousal (as a dimension of emotion), specific emotions (along both the arousal and the valence dimensions), and the population under study (patients vs. fearful participants vs. healthy controls). Further, to fully understand presence in VR and its unique characteristics, the investigation of presence in reality, e.g., during in vivo exposure as compared to VR exposure, appears vital (Seth et al., 2012). We can reasonably assume that, when making sense of a VR environment, people apply the same mechanisms to it as they do to everyday reality (Seth et al., 2012). A direct comparison of both worlds has, unfortunately, long been neglected.

| *"VR is now firmly established as an experimental tool."*

Despite Challenges, VR Offers Opportunities for Psychology Research

Christopher J. Wilson and Alessandro Soranzo

In the following viewpoint, Christopher J. Wilson and Alessandro Soranzo argue that virtual reality offers many advantages as a tool for conducting psychological research over traditional methods. Through VR, researchers can present more realistic, three-dimensional scenarios to subjects to measure behavior change. On the other hand, they acknowledge that there are challenges with the level of presence and immersion felt by research subjects. Wilson is affiliated with Teesside University, and Soranzo is affiliated with Sheffield Hallam University, both in the United Kingdom.

As you read, consider the following questions:

1. According to the authors, what advantages does VR technology have as a research tool in psychology?
2. How have VR avatars been used to measure helping behaviors in experiment participants?
3. What are some of the "virtual reality-induce side effects" caused by being immersed in VR environments?

"The Use of Virtual Reality in Psychology: A Case Study in Visual Perception," Christopher J. Wilson and Alessandro Soranzo, Hindawi Corporation Publishing, 2015. http://www.hindawi.com/journals/cmmm/2015/151702/.

1. Introduction

The proliferation of available virtual reality (VR) tools has seen increased use in experimental psychology settings over the last twenty years [1–4]. For the researcher, VR is compelling due to the almost limitless possibilities for the creation of stimuli and this has led to spread of VR into domains such as clinical and developmental psychology, which one might not have initially anticipated [5–7]. Once considered to be an "answer without a question," VR is now firmly established as an experimental tool [8]. However, in addition to the many advantages associated with the use of VR, there remain some drawbacks and ongoing questions. Of course, the relative importance of these issues is dependent entirely on the use case; while presence may be important in a clinical setting, for example, issues with space perception may limit the accuracy of a physical reach task. Similarly, in the experimental examination of visual perception, potential differences between actual and virtual reality can either be advantageous or detrimental. In this paper we provide a brief overview of the benefits and challenges associated with VR in psychology research and discuss its utility in relation to the examination of visual perception.

The term VR is often used interchangeably to refer to one of three types of system: a virtual environment presented on a flat screen, a room-based system such as a CAVE, or a head-mounted display (HMD: [9, 10]). Though all three systems are quite different, a common feature of all three is the introduction of stereoscopic depth, which creates the illusion that the viewer is seeing objects in a virtual space [11]. This offers a number of immediate advantages to the researcher: greater control over stimulus presentation, variety in response options, and potentially increased ecological validity [12]. This has led to increased use of VR as a research tool across many psychological domains such as psychotherapy [13, 14], sports psychology [15], and social interaction [16].

The most apparent advantage of VR is the ability to present stimuli in three dimensions. This offers specific benefits depending on the research domain. For example, when discussing the potential application of VR to neuropsychological research, Rizzo et al. [17] describe virtual environments as "the ultimate Skinner box," able to present a range of complex stimulus conditions that would not be easily controllable in the real world and enabling the examination of both cognitive processes (e.g., attention) and functional behaviours (e.g., planning and initiating a series of required actions). In clinical research VR is used to create complex scenarios, such as simulating exposure to a phobic stimulus, where the form and frequency of the exposure can be manipulated with absolute precision [4]. These examples highlight the difference between VR stimulus presentation and traditional experimental procedures: in VR the participant responds to pertinent stimuli while immersed in a larger virtual environment which can itself be controlled. This differs from traditional experimental contexts where the pertinent stimuli may be controlled but the surrounding environment often cannot be.

Of course, if VR were only a visual medium, then it could be argued that its only advantage over traditional experimental protocols is the ability to present visual stimuli along a third dimensional plane. However, as VR technology has advanced, many VR research studies now include varying levels and combinations of multimodal sensory input, allowing audio, haptic, olfactory, and motion to be experienced simultaneously to the graphically rendered environment or objects [18–20]. This greatly increases the user's sense of immersion in the virtual environment and allows the experimenter to create protocols that would not otherwise be possible. For example, exposure therapy is a common method employed in the treatment of anxiety disorders which, in the case of PTSD, may be difficult to implement for logistical or safety reasons. To overcome these issues, multimodal VR has been employed to create a virtual replica of a warzone, complete with audio and haptic feedback, to treat PTSD in war veterans [21, 22]. Where phenomena are known to occur due to a confluence of sensory data (e.g., audio and visual), multimodal VR enables the researcher to manipulate each input separately to gain a more accurate understanding of the relative contribution of each. For example, a recent study by Keshavarz et al. [23] employed this technique to assess the effects of auditory and visual cues on the perception of vection and resultant motion sickness in participants. Finally, multimodal environments are associated with faster mental processing times of discrete stimulus events, potentially because they provide the user with more complete information about the environment [24].

In addition to the presentation of experimental stimuli, VR enabled researchers to develop new protocols to measure participant responding. Many researchers have no doubt lamented the situation where studies that aim to assess a complex psychological construct (e.g., attention) have, out of necessity, been reduced to a mere "point and click" exercise for the participant. Most experiments strike a difficult balance between control and ecological validity, and very few replicate the multifaceted nature of real-life human responding [25]. It has been suggested that VR environments might help bridge this gap by allowing participants to respond in a manner that is more natural [26]. This can be seen across a range of psychological topics. For example, studies on altruism or prosocial behaviour are often carried out using hypothetical scenarios and self-report responses [27]. Kozlov and Johansen [2] on the other hand, employed a novel approach to examining this topic using VR. As participants attempted to navigate out of a virtual maze, under time pressure, virtual avatars approached the participant for help in a variety of situations. This enabled the experimenters to measure actual helping behaviours, as opposed to participants reporting what they would hypothetically do in such a situation. The researchers argue that even sophisticated high-level behaviours can be successfully examined using VR and suggest wider adoption. VR environments have also been used recently to examine the avoidance behaviour, a central component of fear that contributes to the maintenance of anxiety disorders. While many studies have examined the physiological and self-report aspects of fear, few have been able to examine the associated avoidance of, for example, the context or environment that elicits the fear response [28]. Glotzbach et al. [29] were able to directly examine avoidance behaviour by conditioning participants to be afraid of particular virtual environments and recording the extent to which they avoided returning to those environments later in the study. Finally, VR could be useful to measure responses in circumstances where it might be impractical or ethically questionable to do so in real life. For example, Renaud et al. [30] used a virtual environment and avatars to examine sexual affordances of convicted child molesters. The VR setup allowed the researchers to identify specific patterns of gaze behaviour exhibited by the experimental and not the control group of participants. They discuss a number of theoretical discussions that emerged from the study by virtue of the "first-person stance" enabled by using VR.

2. Questions About the Use of VR in Psychology Research

Since many of the advantages of VR as an experimental tool are derived from the ability to place the participant inside the scene, it is not surprising that a lot of research has been conducted into the concept of presence—the extent to which the user feels as though they are "really there" [31, 32]. Presence is viewed as crucial to having participants respond the same way in VR as they would in reality but remains a difficult concept to measure objectively [32–34]. Many studies have recorded user's subjective experience of presence and the perceived effect it has on engagement with tasks in a virtual environment [35–38]. Kober and Neuper [39] attempted to measure presence objectively and posit that it is characterised by increased attention toward stimuli in the virtual environment and correspondingly lower attention to VR irrelevant stimuli. They were able to identify distinct ERP patterns associated with increased presence. Furthermore, [32] found differences in the levels of presence elicited by a desktop VR system and a more immersive single-wall VR system, which was characterised by stronger activation of frontal and parietal brain regions, measured using EEG.

One of the determinants of presence is the level of immersion, described as the level of sensory fidelity offered by the VR system [40]. It has many contributing components such as field of view, field of regard, display size, and stereoscopy (not exhaustive) and although many use the terms presence and immersion interchangeably (e.g., [41]), they are very different concepts [31]. Immersion is an objective description of the technical capabilities of the VR system that describes the level of detail with which a virtual environment can be rendered, while presence describes the user's psychological response to said environment. Different users can experience different levels of presence in environment with the same level of immersion, depending on a range of factors such as state of mind. Still, it seems intuitive that a researcher would want higher levels of immersion wherever possible, as a higher-fidelity virtual world would elicit more generalizable responses. Indeed, immersive environments seem to be better remembered by participants [37], elicit more intense emotional responses [42], increase collaboration [43], and more successfully replicate the anxiety associated with real-life stressful situations [44]. At the same time, creating an environment elicits a sense of presence that is not entirely dependent on immersion. Factors such as personality and emotional state also influence presence [45–47]. In a research context, realism might not be determined by visual fidelity but by psychological fidelity: the extent to which stimulus presentation evokes the type of physiological or emotional response one would experience in real life. While immersion might help with this goal, it is not the only determining factor [3].

Indeed, it is not universally accepted that higher immersion is always better with some researchers reporting physical and psychological side effects from exposure to VR. These are collectively referred to as virtual reality-induced side effects (VRISE [48]) and often focus on a general feeling of malaise or perhaps motion sickness experienced by users [49]. The effect was initially believed to be caused by limitations in early VR technologies where there was often a lag between participant movements and the display being updated resulting in a disconnection between the perceptual and motor systems of the user [50]. However, while technological advances have overcome this early limitation, VRISE remain a problem [23, 51, 52]. Although common in most VR users, these side effects vary from person to person and, as such, it is difficult to pin down what aspects of immersion are responsible. While some studies suggest that more immersive HMDs are linked to higher levels of sickness in participants [53], others suggest that there is little difference between the side effects of using standard desktop computer display and a head-mounted VR display [54]. Regardless, it seems that these symptoms are generally mild and quick to subside and there is some evidence that users can adapt with repeated exposure [1, 55–57]. While not all that common in the literature, researchers should also consider potential psychological side effects of VR use, depending on the topic being examined. For example, Aardema et al. [58] found that users who had been exposed to an immersive virtual environment demonstrated increase in dissociative experience including a lessened sense of presence in objective reality as the result of exposure to VR, while Aimé et al. [59] found that VR immersion led to body dissatisfaction amongst users. As VR environments become more realistic and scenarios potentially more complex, another potential confound may arise from what Yee and Bailenson [60] term the Proteus effect, where users in a VR environment change their behaviour depending on how they are represented in the virtual world, though currently this effect seems limited to studies that use third-person view and avatars, as opposed to first person perspective [61].

3. The Use of VR in Visual Perception Research

In many domains, the benefits of VR stem from the ability to create recognisable, three-dimensional facsimiles of real objects in space. As a simplified example, let us imagine a study that asks participants to attend to the environment and respond every time they see a person with a happy face. Here the researcher needs only the object (face) to be presented, to be recognised by the participant, and to measure some level of reaction on the part of the participant. In such a context, the main technical focus in relation to VR is likely to be the visual fidelity of the stimuli—the extent to which the faces can be detailed enough for participants to distinguish their expressions. In the experimental study of visual perception, however, the researcher is concerned with how the stimuli are perceived. Here, VR offers both advantages and drawbacks when compared with real life and traditional experimental apparatus. In the following section, we focus on interesting aspects of immersive VR environments that impact how we examine perception: (1) space and movement and (2) tighter control over the visual scene.

3.1. The Effect of Space and Movement in VR on Perception

One area where complications arise is in the perception of space [62]. Many studies have observed a disparity between judgements of distance and perceptual actions such as reaching [63, 64]. In addition, it has been found that in VR, users consistently underestimate the size of the environment and distance to objects [65]. Although not always replicated (e.g., [66]), this effect has been found to be consistent with binocular and monocular vision [67], with varying field of view [68] and even when providing motion parallax and stereoscopic depth cues to the observer [69]. Bingham et al. [62] provide a useful explanation: what we see in VR as an object is actually a series of images mediated by a display. While the user's vision is focused on the series of images that make up the virtual object, the object itself appears in a different location. As a result, when the user is viewing the object, there is disconnect between accommodation (the fixed viewing distance between the user and the display) and convergence (the user's eyes converging on the virtual object), two processes that are inextricably linked in viewing objects in actual reality. Some studies have suggested that this effect is an issue of perception-action recalibration, while others suggest that walking through the virtual environment with continuous visual feedback is necessary to cause rescaling of the perceived space [70].

On the other hand, there are instances where the disconnection between virtual and actual reality provides opportunities for the examination of perception, which would otherwise not be possible. Mast and Oman [71] used a virtual environment to examine visual reorientation illusions, a phenomenon reported by astronauts where the perceived identity of a surface is changed due to rotation of the entire visual field. This phenomenon is difficult to replicate in real life, as we are surrounded by visual cues in our environment that help us to orient ourselves (e.g., trees grow upwards), as well as the orienting force of gravity, which provides a consistent cue for "down." The authors created an immersive environment (i.e., a room containing various objects) with intentionally ambiguous visual cues so that, due to the placement of objects in the room, it could appear correctly oriented even if the room were rotated by 90°. The researchers were then able to rotate the entire visual scene and examine the effects on perception—something that would be almost impossible to replicate in the physical environment.

In addition to creating new illusions, an immersive environment offers the possibility to examine commonly employed visual illusions in new contexts. Traditionally, illusions to examine perception are designed and employed assuming a stationary point of view and have not been studied thoroughly for a moving observer. By employing an immersive environment it is possible to investigate whether these illusions persist when the observer moves. This would be difficult to carry out using a two-dimensional computer screen setup, due to the fact that the stimuli, and hence the illusion, require the observer to view the screen head on. Bruder et al. [72] introduced the use of VR to investigate how visual motion illusions are perceived for a moving observer. The authors manipulated the optical flow—the change of the light pattern on the observer's eyes when moving in the environment—

and found that optic flow manipulation can significantly affect users' self-motion judgments.

Movement can also add ecological validity to the examination of everyday perceptual phenomena. Change blindness, a phenomenon in which changes occurring in a visual scene are not noticed by the observer, occurs in a variety of contexts and its impact is studied in range of applied settings from courtroom eye-witness testimony to driving behaviour [73, 74]. Experimental examinations of the effect are usually done on a computer screen where two similar images are presented one after the other with a short blanking between the two, and observers have to indicate whether the second image is the same as the first one or if a change has occurred [75]. Using VR to create a more ecologically valid examination of the phenomenon, Suma et al. [76] had the observer walk through an immersive virtual environment and found that even large changes in the surrounding environment were unlikely to be noticed.

3.2. Control over the Visual Scene

Virtual reality technology overcomes a number of the limitations of traditional experimental methods by enabling precise control of the spatial distribution of the light in the visual scene as well as distance and position of stimuli. In a real room, it is not possible to manipulate these elements completely independently. However, with virtual reality it is possible to manipulate the distances between the surfaces whilst at the same time maintaining the same photometric relationships (i.e., the amount of light reaching the observers' eyes remained constant). Furthermore, by manipulating objects in three-dimensional space, it is possible to examine the effects of positive and negative parallax which would not be possible using a two-dimensional screen. Moreover, the VR technology allows full control of the amount of light reaching the observers' eyes and of the spatial arrangement of the surfaces in the visual scene.

This level of control is particularly useful when we examine colour perception and particular visual phenomena such as colour contrast phenomenon [77]. The colour contrast phenomenon refers to the condition whereby two surfaces with the same spectral composition are perceived to have a different colour when they are placed against different chromatic backgrounds. It has been shown that this phenomenon depends on perceptual belongingness, the grouping of a set of apparent elements into a perceived whole [78, 79]. As Gilchrist et al. [80] explained, "When the [contrast] display is presented in a textbook, it is perceived to belong to the page of the book and to the table on which the book is lying. Thus, […] the illusion should be quite weak" (p. 814). Adopting a VR technology prevents surfaces from outside of the experimental display from affecting the experimental examination of the colour contrast phenomenon. Although the contrast phenomenon has been a focus of centuries of debate that has interested scientists and philosophers since Aristotle's time [81], there is still no shared consensus of why it actually happens as some authors attribute its occurrence to high-level factors of the visual process whilst others claim that the phenomenon is due to low-level factors. In an attempt to disentangle these viewpoints, Soranzo et al. [82] studied this phenomenon in VR and provided evidence that the colour contrast phenomenon may be attributed to the summative effect of factors occurring to both high- and low-level factors of the visual process.

4. Conclusions

The proliferation of available virtual reality (VR) tools has seen increased use in experimental psychology settings over the last twenty years. In this review, we outlined the advantages and disadvantages of this technology in psychological research, compared to more traditional apparatus. The advantages of VR are that it allows greater control over stimulus presentation; variety in response options; presentation of stimuli in three dimensions; the creation of complex scenarios; the generation of varying levels and combinations of multimodal sensory input potentially allowing audio, haptic, olfactory, and motion to be experienced simultaneously to the graphically rendered environment or objects; the possibility for participants to respond in a more ecologically valid manner; the precise and independent manipulation of the geometric and photometric relationships between objects; the possibility of examining sophisticated complex participants behaviours, such as avoidance; and the study of situations which can be impractical, dangerous, or ethically questionable to be created in real life.

Additionally, we suggest that although this technology has enormous potential to facilitate new discoveries in psychology, there are certain variables that need to be taken into account by the researcher including the concept of presence—immersion alone is not necessarily sufficient to make the participant feel as if the virtual objects are "really there" and respond accordingly; physical and psychological side effects from exposure to VR (virtual reality-induced side effects). In addition, we considered issues that emerge from use of VR in the examination of visual perception and how comparative differences in the perception of colour, contrast, space, and movement, when compared to real life, can be a concern if the goal is exact replication of perception in the physical world or an advantage when trying to create "impossible scenarios."

Finally, it is worth noting that there are large variations in the size and cost of the various apparatus and in some cases they can be impractical for some settings due to their technological complexities. Until quite recently, the price of immersive HMDs with a good tracker system could be prohibitive. However, HMDs are now becoming cheaper and easier to obtain [83, 84], while virtual reality caves, for example, are still comparatively more expensive and require a large amount of space to install [9, 85]. Nevertheless, VR offers exciting opportunities and we hope to see future work that more thoroughly examines the psychometric properties of this useful research tool.

References

L. Gregg and N. Tarrier, "Virtual reality in mental health: a review of the literature," *Social Psychiatry and Psychiatric Epidemiology*, vol. 42, no. 5, pp. 343–354, 2007.

M. D. Kozlov and M. K. Johansen, "Real behavior in virtual environments: psychology experiments in a simple virtual-reality paradigm using video games," *Cyberpsychology, Behavior, and Social Networking*, vol. 13, no. 6, pp. 711–714, 2010.

S. Schnall, C. Hedge, and R. Weaver, "The immersive virtual environment of the digital fulldome: considerations of relevant psychological processes," *International Journal of Human Computer Studies*, vol. 70, no. 8, pp. 561–575, 2012.

S. Scozzari and L. Gamberini, "Virtual reality as a tool for cognitive behavioral therapy: a review," in *Advanced Computational Intelligence Paradigms in Healthcare 6. Virtual Reality in Psychotherapy, Rehabilitation, and Assessment*, S. Brahnam and L. C. Jain, Eds., vol. 337 of *Studies in Computational Intelligence*, pp. 63–108, Springer, Berlin, Germany, 2011.

G. Rajendran, "Virtual environments and autism: a developmental psychopathological approach," *Journal of Computer Assisted Learning*, vol. 29, no. 4, pp. 334–347, 2013.

G. Riva, "Virtual environments in clinical psychology," *Psychotherapy: Theory, Research, Practice, Training*, vol. 40, no. 1-2, pp. 68–76, 2003.

G. Riva, "Virtual reality in psychotherapy: review," *Cyberpsychology & Behavior*, vol. 8, no. 3, pp. 220–240, 2005.

N. Foreman, "Virtual reality in psychology," *Themes in Science and Technology Education*, vol. 2, no. 1-2, pp. 225–252, 2009.

C. Cruz-Neira, D. J. Sandin, and T. A. DeFanti, "Surround-screen projection-based virtual reality: the design and implementation of the CAVE," in *Proceedings of the ACM Conference on Computer Graphics (SIGGRAPH '93)*, pp. 135–142, August 1993.

R. M. Taylor II, J. Jerald, C. VanderKnyff et al., "Lessons about virtual environment software systems from 20 Years of VE building," *Presence: Teleoperators and Virtual Environments*, vol. 19, no. 2, pp. 162–178, 2010.

J. P. Wann, S. Rushton, and M. Mon-Williams, "Natural problems for stereoscopic depth perception in virtual environments," *Vision Research*, vol. 35, no. 19, pp. 2731–2736, 1995.

Y. P. Zinchenko, G. Y. Men'shikova, Y. M. Bayakovsky, A. M. Chernorizov, and A. E. Voiskounsky, "Technologies of virtual reality in the context of world-wide and Russian psychology: methodology, comparison with traditional methods, achievements and perspectives," *Psychology in Russia: State of the Art*, no. 3, pp. 12–45, 2010.

C. Suied, G. Drettakis, O. Warusfel, and I. Viaud-Delmon, "Auditory-visual virtual reality as a diagnostic and therapeutic tool for cynophobia," *Cyberpsychology, Behavior, and Social Networking*, vol. 16, no. 2, pp. 145–152, 2013.

D. Villani, F. Riva, and G. Riva, "New technologies for relaxation: the role of presence," *International Journal of Stress Management*, vol. 14, no. 3, pp. 260–274, 2007.

Y. P. Zinchenko, G. Y. Menshikova, A. M. Chernorizov, and A. E. Voiskounsky, "Technologies of virtual reality in psychology of sport of great advance: theory, practice and perspectives," *Psychology in Russia: State of the art*, vol. 4, no. 1, pp. 129–154, 2011.

P. R. Messinger, E. Stroulia, K. Lyons et al., "Virtual worlds—past, present, and future: new directions in social computing," *Decision Support Systems*, vol. 47, no. 3, pp. 204–228, 2009.

A. A. Rizzo, M. Schultheis, K. A. Kerns, and C. Mateer, "Analysis of assets for virtual reality applications in neuropsychology," *Neuropsychological Rehabilitation*, vol. 14, no. 1-2, pp. 207–239, 2004.

C. J. Bohil, B. Alicea, and F. A. Biocca, "Virtual reality in neuroscience research and therapy," *Nature Reviews Neuroscience*, vol. 12, no. 12, pp. 752–762, 2011.

G. Burdea, P. Richard, and P. Coiffet, "Multimodal virtual reality: input-output devices, system integration, and human factors," *International Journal of Human-Computer Interaction*, vol. 8, no. 1, pp. 5–24, 1996.

D. Navarre, P. Palanque, R. Bastide et al., "A formal description of multimodal interaction techniques for immersive virtual reality applications," in *Human-Computer Interaction— INTERACT 2005*, vol. 3585 of *Lecture Notes in Computer Science*, pp. 170–183, Springer, Berlin, Germany, 2005.

M. Gerardi, B. O. Rothbaum, K. Ressler, M. Heekin, and A. Rizzo, "Virtual reality exposure therapy using a virtual Iraq: case report," *Journal of Traumatic Stress*, vol. 21, no. 2, pp. 209–213, 2008.

R. J. Nelson, "Is virtual reality exposure therapy effective for service members and veterans experiencing combat-related PTSD?" *Traumatology*, vol. 19, no. 3, pp. 171–178, 2013.

B. Keshavarz, L. J. Hettinger, D. Vena, and J. L. Campos, "Combined effects of auditory and visual cues on the perception of vection," *Experimental Brain Research*, vol. 232, no. 3, pp. 827–836, 2014. ·

D. Hecht, M. Reiner, and G. Halevy, "Multimodal virtual environments: response times, attention, and presence," *Presence: Teleoperators and Virtual Environments*, vol. 15, no. 5, pp. 515–521, 2006.

H. T. Hunt, "Why psychology is/is not traditional science: the self-referential bases of psychological research and theory," *Review of General Psychology*, vol. 9, no. 4, pp. 358–374, 2005.

M. T. Schultheis and A. A. Rizzo, "The application of virtual reality technology in rehabilitation," *Rehabilitation Psychology*, vol. 46, no. 3, pp. 296–311, 2001.

S. M. Garcia, K. Weaver, G. B. Moskowitz, and J. M. Darley, "Crowded minds: the implicit bystander effect," *Journal of Personality and Social Psychology*, vol. 83, no. 4, pp. 843–853, 2002.

C. Grillon, "Associative learning deficits increase symptoms of anxiety in humans," *Biological Psychiatry*, vol. 51, no. 11, pp. 851–858, 2002.

E. Glotzbach, H. Ewald, M. Andreatta, P. Pauli, and A. Mühlberger, "Contextual fear conditioning predicts subsequent avoidance behaviour in a virtual reality environment," *Cognition & Emotion*, vol. 26, no. 7, pp. 1256–1272, 2012.

P. Renaud, S. Chartier, J.-L. Rouleau et al., "Using immersive virtual reality and ecological psychology to probe into child molesters' phenomenology," *Journal of Sexual Aggression*, vol. 19, no. 1, pp. 102–120, 2013.

D. A. Bowman and R. P. McMahan, "Virtual reality: how much immersion is enough?" *Computer*, vol. 40, no. 7, pp. 36–43, 2007.

S. E. Kober, J. Kurzmann, and C. Neuper, "Cortical correlate of spatial presence in 2D and 3D interactive virtual reality: an EEG study," *International Journal of Psychophysiology*, vol. 83, no. 3, pp. 365–374, 2012.

J. V. Draper, D. B. Kaber, and J. M. Usher, "Speculations on the value of telepresence," *CyberPsychology and Behavior*, vol. 2, no. 4, pp. 349–362, 1999.

M. Slater, B. Lotto, M. M. Arnold, and M. V. Sanchez-Vives, "How we experience immersive virtual environments: the concept of presence and its measurement," *Anuario de Psicologia*, vol. 40, no. 2, pp. 193–210, 2009.

E. Giannopoulos, Z. Wang, A. Peer, M. Buss, and M. Slater, "Comparison of people's responses to real and virtual handshakes within a virtual environment," *Brain Research Bulletin*, vol. 85, no. 5, pp. 276–282, 2011.

R. Ma and D. B. Kaber, "Presence, workload and performance effects of synthetic environment design factors," *International Journal of Human Computer Studies*, vol. 64, no. 6, pp. 541–552, 2006.

A. Sutcliffe, B. Gault, and J.-E. Shin, "Presence, memory and interaction in virtual environments," *International Journal of Human Computer Studies*, vol. 62, no. 3, pp. 307–327, 2005.

S. Sylaiou, K. Mania, A. Karoulis, and M. White, "Exploring the relationship between presence and enjoyment in a virtual museum," *International Journal of Human Computer Studies*, vol. 68, no. 5, pp. 243–253, 2010.

S. E. Kober and C. Neuper, "Using auditory event-related EEG potentials to assess presence in virtual reality," *International Journal of Human Computer Studies*, vol. 70, no. 9, pp. 577–587, 2012.

M. Slater, "A note on presence terminology," *Emotion*, vol. 3, pp. 1–5, 2003.

A. M. Grinberg, J. S. Careaga, M. R. Mehl, and M.-F. O'Connor, "Social engagement and user immersion in a socially based virtual world," *Computers in Human Behavior*, vol. 36, pp. 479–486, 2014.

V. T. Visch, E. S. Tan, and D. Molenaar, "The emotional and cognitive effect of immersion in film viewing," *Cognition and Emotion*, vol. 24, no. 8, pp. 1439–1445, 2010.

J.-M. Burkhardt, "Immersion, représentation et coopération : discussion et perspectives de recherches empiriques pour l'ergonomie cognitive de la réalité virtuelle," *Intellectica*, vol. 45, no. 1, pp. 59–87, 2007.

J. H. Kwon, J. Powell, and A. Chalmers, "How level of realism influences anxiety in virtual reality environments for a job interview," *International Journal of Human-Computer Studies*, vol. 71, no. 10, pp. 978–987, 2013.

Y. Ling, H. T. Nefs, W.-P. Brinkman, C. Qu, and I. Heynderickx, "The relationship between individual characteristics and experienced presence," *Computers in Human Behavior*, vol. 29, no. 4, pp. 1519–1530, 2013.

M. Rubin and T. Morrison, "Individual differences in individualism and collectivism predict ratings of virtual cities' liveability and environmental quality," *The Journal of General Psychology*, vol. 141, no. 4, pp. 348–372, 2014.

S. Triberti, C. Repetto, and G. Riva, "Psychological factors influencing the effectiveness of virtual reality-based analgesia: a systematic review," *Cyberpsychology, Behavior, and Social Networking*, vol. 17, no. 6, pp. 335–345, 2014.

S. Sharples, S. Cobb, A. Moody, and J. R. Wilson, "Virtual reality induced symptoms and effects (VRISE): comparison of head mounted display (HMD), desktop and projection display systems,"*Displays*, vol. 29, no. 2, pp. 58–69, 2008.

A. Murata, "Effects of duration of immersion in a virtual reality environment on postural stability," *International Journal of Human-Computer Interaction*, vol. 17, no. 4, pp. 463–477, 2004.

F. Biocca, "Will simulation sickness slow down the diffusion of virtual environment technology?" *Presence: Teleoperators and Virtual Environments*, vol. 1, no. 3, pp. 334–343, 1992.

P. A. Howarth and S. G. Hodder, "Characteristics of habituation to motion in a virtual environment,"*Displays*, vol. 29, no. 2, pp. 117–123, 2008.

N. Sugita, M. Yoshizawa, A. Tanaka et al., "Quantitative evaluation of effects of visually-induced motion sickness based on causal coherence functions between blood pressure and heart rate," *Displays*, vol. 29, no. 2, pp. 167–175, 2008.

J. Moss, J. Scisco, and E. Muth, "Simulator sickness during head mounted display (HMD) of real world video captured scenes," in *Proceedings of the Human Factors and Ergonomics Society Annual Meeting*, vol. 52, pp. 1631–1634, 2008.

E. Peli, "The visual effects of head-mounted display (HMD) are not distinguishable from those of desk-top computer display," *Vision Research*, vol. 38, no. 13, pp. 2053–2066, 1998.

K. J. Hill and P. A. Howarth, "Habituation to the side effects of immersion in a virtual environment,"*Displays*, vol. 21, no. 1, pp. 25–30, 2000.

S. Nichols and H. Patel, "Health and safety implications of virtual reality: a review of empirical evidence," *Applied Ergonomics*, vol. 33, no. 3, pp. 251–271, 2002.

E. C. Regan, "Some evidence of adaptation to immersion in virtual reality," *Displays*, vol. 16, no. 3, pp. 135–139, 1995.

F. Aardema, K. O'Connor, S. Côté, and A. Taillon, "Virtual reality induces dissociation and lowers sense of presence in objective reality," *Cyberpsychology, Behavior, and Social Networking*, vol. 13, no. 4, pp. 429–435, 2010.

A. Aimé, K. Cotton, and S. Bouchard, "Reactivity to VR immersions in women with weight and shape concerns," *Journal of Cyber Therapy and Rehabilitation*, vol. 2, no. 2, pp. 115–126, 2009.

N. Yee and J. Bailenson, "The proteus effect: the effect of transformed self-representation on behavior," *Human Communication Research*, vol. 33, no. 3, pp. 271–290, 2007.

N. Yee, J. N. Bailenson, and N. Ducheneaut, "The proteus effect: implications of transformed digital self-representation on online and offline behavior," *Communication Research*, vol. 36, no. 2, pp. 285–312, 2009.

G. P. Bingham, A. Bradley, M. Bailey, and R. Vinner, "Accommodation, occlusion, and disparity matching are used to guide reaching: a comparison of actual versus virtual environments," *Journal of Experimental Psychology: Human Perception and Performance*, vol. 27, no. 6, pp. 1314–1334, 2001.

S. Aglioti, J. F. X. DeSouza, and M. A. Goodale, "Size-contrast illusions deceive the eye but not the hand," *Current Biology*, vol. 5, no. 6, pp. 679–685, 1995.

J. C. Baird and W. R. Biersdorf, "Quantitative functions for size and distance judgments," *Perception & Psychophysics*, vol. 2, no. 4, pp. 161–166, 1967.

V. Interrante, B. Ries, J. Lindquist, M. Kaeding, and L. Anderson, "Elucidating factors that can facilitate veridical spatial perception in immersive virtual environments," *Presence: Teleoperators and Virtual Environments*, vol. 17, no. 2, pp. 176–198, 2008.

J. W. Kelly, A. C. Beall, and J. M. Loomis, "Perception of shared visual space: establishing common ground in real and virtual environments," *Presence: Teleoperators and Virtual Environments*, vol. 13, no. 4, pp. 442–450, 2004.

D. R. Melmoth and S. Grant, "Advantages of binocular vision for the control of reaching and grasping," *Experimental Brain Research*, vol. 171, no. 3, pp. 371–388, 2006.

J. M. Knapp and J. M. Loomis, "Limited field of view of head-mounted displays is not the cause of distance underestimation in virtual environments," *Presence: Teleoperators and Virtual Environments*, vol. 13, no. 5, pp. 572–577, 2004.

I. V. Piryankova, S. de la Rosa, U. Kloos, H. H. Bülthoff, and B. J. Mohler, "Egocentric distance perception in large screen immersive displays," *Displays*, vol. 34, no. 2, pp. 153–164, 2013.

J. W. Kelly, L. S. Donaldson, L. A. Sjolund, and J. B. Freiberg, "More than just perception-action recalibration: walking through a virtual environment causes rescaling of perceived space," *Attention, Perception, and Psychophysics*, vol. 75, no. 7, pp. 1473–1485, 2013.

F. W. Mast and C. M. Oman, "Top-down processing and visual reorientation illusions in a virtual reality environment," *Swiss Journal of Psychology*, vol. 63, no. 3, pp. 143–149, 2004.

G. Bruder, F. Steinicke, P. Wieland, and M. Lappe, "Tuning self-motion perception in virtual reality with visual illusions," *IEEE Transactions on Visualization and Computer Graphics*, vol. 18, no. 7, pp. 1068–1078, 2012.

S. G. Charlton and N. J. Starkey, "Driving on familiar roads: automaticity and inattention blindness," *Transportation Research Part F: Traffic Psychology and Behaviour*, vol. 19, pp. 121–133, 2013.

R. J. Fitzgerald, C. Oriet, and H. L. Price, "Change blindness and eyewitness identification: effects on accuracy and confidence," *Legal and Criminological Psychology*, 2014.

G. W. McConkie and C. B. Currie, "Visual stability across saccades while viewing complex pictures," *Journal of Experimental Psychology: Human Perception and Performance*, vol. 22, no. 3, pp. 563–581, 1996.

E. A. Suma, S. Clark, S. L. Finkelstein, and Z. Wartell, "Exploiting change blindness to expand walkable space in a virtual environment," in *IEEE Virtual Reality Conference (VR '10)*, pp. 305–306, March 2010.

G. Y. Menshikova, "An investigation of 3D images of the simultaneous-lightnesscontrast illusion using a virtual-reality technique," *Psychology in Russia: State of the Art*, vol. 6, no. 3, pp. 49–59, 2013.

W. Benary, "Beobachtungen zu einem Experiment über Helligkeitskontrast," *Psychologische Forschung*, vol. 5, no. 1, pp. 131–142, 1924.

M. Wertheimer, "Untersuchungen zur Lehre von der Gestalt. II," *Psychologische Forschung*, vol. 4, no. 1, pp. 301–350, 1923.

A. Gilchrist, C. Kossyfidis, F. Bonato, et al., "An anchoring theory of lightness perception," *Psychological Review*, vol. 106, no. 4, pp. 795–834, 1999.

N. J. Wade, "Descriptions of visual phenomena from Aristotle to Wheatstone," *Perception*, vol. 25, no. 10, pp. 1137–1175, 1996.

A. Soranzo, J.-L. Lugrin, and C. J. Wilson, "The effects of belongingness on the simultaneous lightness contrast: a virtual reality study," *Vision Research*, vol. 86, pp. 97–106, 2013.

Oculus, Oculus Rift-Virtual Reality Headset for 3D Gaming, 2012, https://www.oculus.com/.

Samsung, Samsung Gear V.R., 2014, http://www.samsung.com/global/microsite/gearvr.

N. Firth, "First wave of virtual reality games will let you live the dream," *New Scientist*, vol. 218, no. 2922, pp. 19–20, 2013.

> *"If violent acts are unsettling in VR, then developers need to learn how to handle its weight; how to direct it, humanise it."*

VR Violent Video Games Could Be Dangerous

Thomas McMullan

In the following viewpoint, Thomas McMullan argues that playing violent games in virtual reality feels entirely different than playing on a screen. He contends that many users will feel almost the same emotions committing violent acts in VR as they would in real life. He suggests that developers should have ethical considerations when creating first-person violent applications. McMullan is a staff writer at Alphr.

As you read, consider the following questions:

1. According to Thomas McMullan, how is playing a violent game in virtual reality different than on a traditional gaming platform?
2. According to the author, what was the purpose of conducting the Milgram experiment in virtual reality?
3. What does the author think are ethical considerations that might occur when playing first-person violent games?

"Virtual Reality Will Change the Way You Think About Violence," Thomas McMullan, Alphr.com. Reprinted by permission.

S it down with a controller and violence happens automatically, absent-mindedly, mathematically. Killing mushrooms, aliens, orcs and soldiers has less to do with murder and more to do with the x and y of gameplay. Even calling it murder sounds ridiculous —something a slapstick vicar might say, monocle popping at the sight of *Mortal Kombat*.

Virtual reality, with the sense of presence it provides, has the potential to completely change all of this—bringing potency to the smallest disturbances and upending the fundamental incongruence between button mashing and the basic physicality of violent acts.

"In a normal game there's an enormous amount of dissonance between what's happening onscreen and what you're experiencing," says George Kelion, communications manager for VR studio nDreams. "You're not really in the experience, you're witnessing the experience—it's secondhand almost. I think violence is entertaining when you can highlight that disconnect.

"The idea of putting a bullet in the back of somebody's head in VR—I think that's something that's far less entertaining and induces much more of an emotional reaction," he adds.

nDreams is currently working on *The Assembly*, a virtual-reality game that tells the story of a secret organisation experimenting outside of governmental or moral restrictions. While the full narrative of the game is under wraps, Kelion walks me through a demo scene where you see a scientist at a banquet table. You enter. The lights go out. When the lights return, the scientist—you later discover it's a mannequin—has two knives sticking out of his back.

Kelion impresses on me that *The Assembly* is not a violent game, but that scene is nevertheless shocking. What would be little more than a minor set-piece decoration in a "flatscreen" game becomes an affecting crescendo in VR. Immersed in the scene, the dissonance between what you're seeing onscreen and what you're experiencing is reduced. You have a physical reaction.

The Milgram Experiment in VR

The Stanley Milgram obedience experiment, originally carried out in the 1960s, examined the conditions in which a subject could be encouraged by an authority figure to harm another human being. In its most famous configuration, the subject would be under the impression they were testing a "learner's" ability to memorise and recite word pairs. If the learner—hidden behind a screen—got the answer wrong, the subject would be told to administer an electric shock.

The voltage would be increased with each wrong answer. As the shocks became more powerful, the learner would complain and eventually urge the subject to stop. An "experimenter," seemingly in charge of the proceedings, would tell the subject to continue. In reality, there were no shocks and the learner was an actor. Rather than memory, the experiment was set up to test whether people would perform acts that went against their personal conscience when ordered to do so by an authority figure. It turned out a very high proportion of people were prepared to obey.

In 2006, researchers from UCL and the University of Barcelona replicated the Milgram experiment within a virtual reality environment. The purpose of this version was not to explore obedience but, as a paper written by the researchers explains, "to use the paradigm to explore the extent to which people would exhibit signs of realistic response, in particular stress at giving the shocks to a virtual character."

The experiment was conducted in a CAVE-like system— essentially a room with projections on three walls and the floor —with the use of 3D glasses and head-tracking. Importantly, the subjects were to feel immersed in the scene. Unlike the original experiment, the subjects were split into two groups: the "visible" group, who sat face to face with a virtual "learner," and a "hidden" group, who largely interacted with the virtual "learner" via text. Analysing the skin conductance, heart rate and heart-rate variability of the subjects, the researchers observed that "the results showed that those in the visible group became more physically aroused and with greater stress than those in the hidden group."

Virtual Self Can Affect Reality Self

Sounds like avatars are for fun and games but could avatars actually change us? Jeremy Bailenson thinks so. With support from the National Science Foundation (NSF), he created the VHIL to study, among other things, the power avatars exert on their real world masters...

Bailenson gives an example. "I use algorithms to age a 20-year-old undergraduate's avatar and then I give that undergraduate the opportunity to save money or to spend it frivolously. The undergraduate will put more money in savings as opposed to go out and spend it on partying."

Your avatar also may affect your fitness. In another test, Del Rosario puts on a head-mounted display that reveals an avatar that looks just like her. As she runs in place, her avatar runs, too, and visibly loses weight. When Del Rosario stands still, her avatar stops, and gets fatter...

"So, the power comes from seeing yourself in the third person gaining and losing weight in accordance with your own physical behavior," says Bailenson. "Twenty-four hours later, people exercised more after being exposed to watching themselves run than watching someone else run."

"Virtual Self Can Affect Reality Self," Miles O'Brien and Ann Kellan, Phys.org., January 24, 2011.

While the researchers avoid making premature conclusions based on one experiment, they do attest to the strength of the subjects' emotional reaction despite the low-quality VR: they say that the virtual learner "did not look like a realistic human, and did not behave like one" but that, nevertheless, "the physiological and emotional responses to the situation were strong."

Providing a Physical Reaction

Giving the player a physical reaction is indeed one of VR's big promises. It's no coincidence that much of the sensationalist reaction around virtual reality has been drawn to areas that hinge on providing an effect: horror and porn. Indeed, it's sensationalism in a very literal sense: this will get your heart racing. This will make you jump out of your seat. This will make you orgasm. In *Kitchen*, a tech demo by Capcom for PlayStation VR, you are tied to a chair as you watch another person try to cut you loose. That person is decapitated off-screen, his head rolls past, and then a *Ring*-like spirit stabs you in the leg. Your brain is tricked into feeling like you're there, and when the knife goes in, it's hard not to wince.

There are, however, necessary ethical questions to consider when shifting the player emphasis from a passive to an active role. What happens if the player takes a more active role? What if the knife is in their hand instead of their leg?

"I'm expecting to see Fox News go a little wild with this at some point," Dan Page, organiser of VR World Congress and VR consultant for Opposable Games, tells me. "Considering virtual reality has been used to treat PTSD sufferers by bringing them back to difficult and violent situations from their past, and to help people out with drug problems via repeated exposure to drug-filled virtual parties, there's no denying that the sense of presence is convincing enough to have some effect on a user."

I ask Page how these concerns are being felt by VR game developers, and he points me towards recent comments by Guerrilla Games developer Piers Jackson, who spoke to Wired about the studio's choice to exclude death from their upcoming VR game *RIGS*. Now, when players fighting in the game's mechanical exoskeletons are defeated, they no longer "die" but are instead ejected to safety. Page also mentioned a recent article in Engadget, where the author spoke about how unsettling it was to see another real-life player kill themselves in *Hover Junkers*, citing the realistic body language of other players despite the game's cartoonish aesthetic. "Whether he's one in a thousand people that might react like that we're yet to see. There's a lot of conjecture and opportunist noise on these kind of matters right now," added Page.

There is indeed a lot of guesswork about the psychological impact of virtual reality, and for an industry teetering on the mass commercial release of its hardware, it's an understandably sensitive issue. Decrying the negative psychological effects of VR without clear empirical evidence would be to miss the point, however. That VR can set off bodily reactions in its players, tricking the brain with a low latency and a wide field of view, is an enormous benefit to developers. From a director's point of view, it means you can do a lot more with a lot less, and tease out strong emotional reactions from subtle environmental detail as much as you can from combat.

Rethinking Violence

"In some ways the VR headset allows us to get at certain instinctive feelings," games writer Rob Morgan tells me. "In a flatscreen game, you have to work really hard and create a whole atmosphere to get to that moment the hair prickles on your neck. You can get to that stuff much more easily in a VR headset, in the same way that a real-life haunted house can creep you out even if it's less convincing than a horror film. You feel more present and it has a closer access to your body's chemistry."

Morgan, who has worked on a number of VR titles including nDreams' *The Assembly*, tells me that immersion is also about the absence of other stimulation. When you're sitting with a controller in your living room, your peripheral vision anchors you in the space. With a headset on your head, there is nowhere else to turn, and this immersive setup lends itself to slower and more contemplative experiences—not least because running at the speed of a traditional first-person shooter tends to incite nausea.

"We're seeing games that actually don't have violence as their central premise, and part of the reason for that is violence in VR does feel different," Morgan tells me. "Violence is never what games were. Play is like a liquid, you can keep putting it in the same bottle but that doesn't mean that's what shape play is. It's just that when you have a controller and TV in front of you, that lends itself to action, to competitiveness."

It's pleasing to think of VR is a different bottle; a different shape for play to take, and yet I'd argue that violence should be a part of the palette used by VR developers, just as it's a crucial part of games such as *Everybody's Gone to the Rapture* and *Firewatch*.

Just because these games emphasise narrative and environment over action doesn't mean they're non-violent. There is palpable violence in both the deserted village of Yaughton and the Wyoming wilderness, as there can be violence in a letter, or a bird, or a room, or a look.

Violence is a part of human nature, not to mention human drama. It's not a matter of avoiding it, therefore, but deepening our approach to it. If violent acts are unsettling in VR, then developers need to learn how to handle its weight; how to direct it, humanise it. Because by bringing our bodies into play, virtual reality has an opportunity to facilitate games that put people under the microscope, not just at the end of a crosshair.

> "*The safety of a virtual experience … can create an encouraging and rewarding environment that is free of the many factors that discourage people from pursuing their dreams.*"

In the Classroom, Virtual Reality Is Better than Real World

Mathew Georghiou

In the following viewpoint, Mathew Georghiou argues that virtual experience is more effective that conventional experiential learning. He contends that among the advantages of VR are its low risk, its ability to manipulate cause and effect, and its motivating qualities. He acknowledges that there are some limitations, but that the benefits outweigh its disadvantages. Georghiou is the CEO and Chief Experience Designer of MediaSpark, Inc.

As you read, consider the following questions:

1. According to Mathew Georghiou, what are some advantages to using virtual reality in learning environments?
2. What does the author think are the benefits of using VR applications as an assessment tool?
3. What does the author think might be potential limitations to using VR in schools?

"9 ways virtual experience beats real-world experience," Mathew Georghiou, Mediaspark. Reprinted by permission.

Experiential learning (learning by doing) is a hot topic these days and getting hotter. I've been evangelizing the benefits of experiential learning for over a decade. But, as much as I believe in the power of experiential learning, it's important to recognize its limitations.

There are two ways to learn by doing: We can gain experience in the real world through our daily activities, or we can gain experience virtually in an activity, game, simulation, or virtual world.

Intuitively, we might automatically believe that there is no substitute for gaining experience in the real world. But, further investigation leads to a different conclusion. Virtual experience can, in fact, be much more effective.

Let's compare:

- With virtual experience, there is no risk. No danger. No loss of money or resources (other than the cost of designing and doing the activity). Minimal loss of time. Not so in the real world.
- With virtual experience, we can succeed through failure. The effectiveness of trial and error should not be underestimated. It's often said that we learn more from our failures than we do from our successes. Perhaps it's because we tend to do more analysis when we fail. Or that the emotional toll it takes on us makes the experience more memorable and drives us to avoid it in the future (as some brain research suggests). In any event, failure in the real world has consequences that discourage or prevent us from even trying.
- With virtual experience, we can simulate any condition we want. For example, how can a pilot learn to fly an airplane in poor weather conditions? Does he jump into a real plane and go looking for a storm? How does he learn to fly with mechanical failure? You get the point.
- With virtual experience, we can control and accelerate the timing of events. Not so in the real world. For example, as a business owner, how long would it take you to experience customer, human resource, financial, and other issues before

A Life-changing Technology

Reducing errors made during surgery, bringing school books to life, enabling us to browse shops from the comfort of home—virtual reality is not just about gaming, it will change our lives, according to some tech leaders [...]

While virtual reality devices put users in fantasy worlds, augmented reality overlays holograms on an actual view.

"What we learn from textbooks or labs can be really dull, but VR and AR will greatly enhance learning abilities," Zhu Bo, founder of InnoValley, a Chinese start-up investor based in Shenzhen, told AFP.

"It can also be used in e-commerce. In the future, you will step into a real scene, you can see the products on the shelves, touch and feel them. So our shopping experience will totally change," said Zhu, who has invested in the field but did not give details [...]

"Believe the Hype? How Virtual Reality Could Change Your Life," Michelle Yun, Phys.org, June 2, 2016.

you gained the wisdom to anticipate and avoid such problems in the future? Would it take months, years, decades?

- With virtual experience, we can isolate and exaggerate cause and effect. In the real world, the consequences of our decisions (and indecisions) may not be easily apparent. They may be hidden from view, or they may be influenced by an endless number of other variables. For example, let's say you invest in a stock, but the value of the stock falls within days of your purchase. Does this mean that something has gone wrong with the company? Or that you chose to invest in the wrong stock? Are all stocks bad? Perhaps it is the economy? If we cannot recognize and evaluate cause and effect, how can we truly learn how the world works?

- With virtual experience, we can guide the learner towards making the correct conclusions. In the real world, our brain is constantly making connections and conclusions, whether we realize it or not. And some of those conclusions are plain wrong (or at the very least, based on insufficient data). For example, if ice-cream sales increase during crime sprees in Central Park, does that mean eating ice-cream encourages criminal activity? Closer investigation might reveal that weather is the driver, not the ice-cream. But, how can we even know when we are coming to incorrect conclusions? It takes a very well-trained mind to see the world objectively, and few people have this ability.

- Virtual experience can be personalized and measured. Learner strengths and weaknesses can be captured and used to guide the learner towards overcoming deficiencies while refining existing skills. Performance can be directly monitored and assessed in an accurate, authentic, and meaningful way. The inefficient and subjective trial-and-error, multiple-choice testing, and peer-review methods used in the real world pale in comparison. And, as the saying goes, "you can't manage what you can't measure."

- Virtual experience can be highly motivating. The real world often delivers significant emotional consequences to a learner, including stress, loss of self-esteem, loss of time, money, and more. I remember hating my first day on the job at IBM. But, eventually, the job turned out great and shaped my life. What if I had quit on that first day? The safety of a virtual experience, combined with well-designed gamification techniques, can create an encouraging and rewarding environment that is free of the many factors that discourage people from pursuing their dreams.

- Virtual experience can be highly scalable and widely accessible. Potentially millions of people can participate in a virtual experience at the same time, at a comparatively minimal cost. It's pretty well impossible to conjure up the massive amounts of time, money, and resources needed to make meaningful real-world experience available to the masses.

To me, that's a pretty convincing list of benefits.

Of course, there are limitations to virtual experience as well. Not everything can be simulated in an effective way. (Hey, if you want to learn how to ride a bike, at some point you are going to have to get on a real bike and start peddling.)

It may also be argued that the designer of the virtual experience may be able to knowingly, or unknowingly, apply undue influence, incorrect data, or subliminal messaging into the learning experience. True. But the same can be said of all other educational methods and the real world too.

Virtual experiences have many advantages, and as technology and education continue to evolve, I continue to believe these types of experiences are going to revolutionize learning as we know it.

Periodical and Internet Sources Bibliography

The following articles have been selected to supplement the diverse views presented in this chapter.

Enrique P. Becerra and Mary Ann Stutts, "Ugly Duckling by Day, Super Model by Night: The Influence of Body Image on the Use of Virtual Worlds," *Journal of Virtual Worlds Research*, November 2008.

Stephanie Castillo, "Planned Parenthood's Virtual Reality Film, 'Across the Line,' Could Help Change Protesters' Behavior," *Medical Daily*, June, 21, 2016.

Michelle R. Kandalaft, Nyaz Didehbani, Daniel C. Krawczyk, Tandra T. Allen, and Sandra B. Chapman, "Virtual Reality Social Cognition Training for Young Adults with High-Functioning Autism," *Journal of Autism and Developmental Disorders,* January 2013.

Michail Kizlov and Mark K. Johansen, "Real Behavior in Virtual Environments: Psychology Experiments in a Simple Virtual-Reality Paradigm Using Video Games," *Cyberpsychology, Behavior, and Social Networking,* December 2010.

Ben Lang, "Exploring AR and VR's Potential: Education and Changing Human Behavior with Virtual Experiences," *Road to VR*, July 18, 2014.

Jack Nicas and Deepa Seetharaman, "What Does Virtual Reality Do to Your Body and Mind?," *Wall Street Journal*, January 3, 2016.

Robin S. Rosenberg, Shawnee L. Baughman, and Jeremy N. Bailenson, "Virtual Superheroes: Using Superpowers in Virtual Reality to Encourage Prosocial Behavior," *PLOS One*, January 30, 2013.

Alexandra Sifferlin, "From World of Warcraft to Weight Loss: How Virtual Reality Can Change Behavior," *TIME*, July 1, 2013.

Paul Solman, "How Virtual Reality Games Can Impact Society, Encourage Prosperity," *PBS News Hour*, July 11, 2013.

Tiffanie Wen, "Can Virtual Reality Make You a Better Person?" BBC, October 1, 2014.

Nick Yee and Jeremy Bailenson, "The Proteus Effect: The Effect of Transformed Self-Representation on Behavior," *Human Communication Research*, 2007.

OPPOSING
VIEWPOINTS®
SERIES

CHAPTER 4

Will Virtual Reality Lead to a Decline in Society?

Chapter Preface

In 2014, when Facebook CEO Mark Zuckerberg announced that his company had just bought virtual reality company Oculus VR, many people in the gaming world became excited. They wondered what the company that had used social media to connect the world would do with the ability to create simulated worlds. Technology experts talked about the intersection of realistic avatars and social media. They did not doubt that VR was going to be the next new technology breakthrough. Though virtual reality has progressed slowly over the last decade, developers have been getting closer to bringing this new digital media into people's everyday lives.

Digital devices have become so ubiquitous that almost no one in the U.S. or Europe would be without a smartphone during the course of their day. People use their devices for work and entertainment, seamlessly switching among apps as though the phone was part of them. Experts in the technology and psychology fields have identified issues of overuse for some smartphone users. They use the terms "addiction" and "dependence" to describe people whose whole lives center around the game and social media apps on their devices. Some experts are concerned that device-dependent people are losing the ability to connect with real people in meaningful ways. They also wonder about the impact of virtual reality, which has the potential to be even more attractive than the two dimensional applications already in use.

Because virtual reality is relatively new, there is still a lot of guesswork about the psychological and societal effects. Researchers have always studied people who excessively use and abuse different means of escaping the demands of everyday life. A small minority of people descend into addictions, and employment and relationships fall by the wayside. Some experts suggest that virtual reality might prove to be too attractive for some people who might choose to spend more time in virtual worlds than real worlds. They might stop needing or craving real social interactions, as virtual ones come without difficult feelings such as awkwardness or embarrassment.

Some users might even prefer a virtual family over marriage and parenthood in the physical world.

Psychologists have monitored heavy users of violent video games to see if the intense content might desensitize the users to violence in real life. The conclusions they have drawn are conflicting and controversial. Some experts speculate that virtual reality may have the potential to cause even more feelings of disconnection among game players. There is particular concern for those people who have risk factors such as antisocial behavior, depression, and poor grades or unemployment. VR games, experts warn, may increase aggressive or criminal behavior.

Not everyone predicts that virtual reality applications will harm society. Many people point out the positive benefits that VR may offer to individuals and groups. Children can take virtual field trips across continents. Infirm grandparents can virtually visit grandchildren across the country. Worshippers can gather together for virtual church services. Exhausted workers can refresh in virtual wildernesses. The possibilities, say VR developers, are endless. The frightening effects can be controlled by self-imposed boundaries in creating the applications and responsible regulations imposed by the government.

The following viewpoints express a range of opinions about the potential for virtual reality to harm society. Whether the risks outweigh the benefits or vice versa is beside the point, most of the authors agree. Virtual reality is here and will become immensely popular, they predict. Becoming informed is the first step to understanding and responsibly using this new, exciting technology.

> *"VR technology will eventually change not only our general image of humanity but also our understanding of deeply entrenched notions."*

VR Developers Must Adhere to a Code of Ethics

Daniel Oberhaus

In the following viewpoint, Daniel Oberhaus argues that the virtual reality industry needs to address the ethical concerns that arise from research and personal use of VR. He claims that there are risks to users of VR and offers recommendations for minimizing them. He acknowledges that there is no regulatory body to enforce or regulate the industry. Daniel Oberhaus is a contributor to Motherboard, *part of Vice Media.*

"We're Already Violating Virtual Reality's First Code of Ethics," Daniel Oberhaus, *Motherboard*, March 6, 2016. Reprinted by permission.

As you read, consider the following questions:

1. According to Daniel Oberhaus, why did Michael Madary and Thomas Metzinger create a code of ethics as a guide for developers of VR applications?
2. What are some of the recommendations Madary and Metzinger made to VR developers?
3. According to the author, what is a challenge that Madary and Mezinger face in getting their recommendations adopted?

It seems as though the advent of any radically new technology is inevitably accompanied by a mad scramble to legislate its proper and improper uses. Whether it's nuclear fission and the IAEA's Convention on Nuclear Safety, or modern medicine and the Hippocratic Oath, these new technologies are seldom allowed to remain morally ambiguous for long.

As such it should come as no surprise that a first stab has already been made at establishing a code of ethics for the burgeoning virtual reality (VR) industry, which will see companies such as Oculus, HTC, and Sony all releasing virtual reality headsets in the coming months. Published last month in *Frontiers in Robotics and AI*, the goal of this pioneering paper was "to present a first list of ethical concerns that may arise from research and personal use of virtual reality and related technology, and to offer concrete recommendations for minimizing those risks."

Written by Michael Madary and Thomas Metzinger, two philosophers from Germany's Johannes Gutenberg University of Mainz, the code of ethics serves as an important counterpoint to all the hype centered on virtual reality's clinical or educational benefits by examining the risks of inhabiting a virtual surrogate body. The duo is particularly looking at immersive virtual reality and the risks run by users when they are subjected to "illusions of embodiment," or feelings of inhabiting a body that is not one's own (like when playing as an avatar in virtual reality, for instance).

"Traditional paradigms in experimental psychology, watching a film, or playing a non-immersive video game cannot create the strong illusion of owning and controlling a body that is not your own," Madary and Metzinger write. "VR technology will eventually change not only our general image of humanity but also our understanding of deeply entrenched notions, such as 'conscious experience,' 'selfhood,' 'authenticity,' or 'realness.'"

As the researchers point out, there is good reason to be especially concerned about the influence of virtual reality on the human brain, as opposed to television or non-immersive video games. A host of psychology experiments have demonstrated the plasticity of the human mind and its unconscious molding by its environment (see the Stanford Prison Experiment or Milgram's obedience experiments for particularly bleak evidence of this).

Yet as efficacious as these experiments have been in showing the susceptibility of the human mind to external cues, none have even come close to amount of environmental control that will hypothetically be possible as virtual reality systems become more ubiquitous.

"Unlike other forms of media, VR can create a situation in which the user's *entire environment* is determined by the creators of the virtual world," Madary and Metzinger write. "[This] introduces opportunities for new and especially powerful forms of both mental and behavioral manipulation, especially when commercial, political, religious, or governmental interests are behind the creation and maintenance of the virtual worlds."

Moreover, a handful of recent experiments have shown that virtual reality experiences have lasting effects even after users have left a virtual environment. Take for instance the virtual reality users who played as a Superman-like avatar and as such were more likely to demonstrate altruistic behavior after leaving the environment, or the virtual reality users who used an avatar with lighter or darker skin who showed a decrease in racial bias after leaving the environment.

Indeed, it was in light of this potential for lasting psychological impact during and after a virtual reality experience that Madary and Metzinger drafted a list of six main recommendations for the ethical future of commercial and research virtual reality applications. Broadly summarized, their recommendations are:

1. In keeping with the American Psychological Association's principle of non-maleficence, experiments using virtual reality should ensure that they do not cause lasting or serious harm to the subject.

2. Subjects participating in experiments using virtual reality should be informed about the lasting and serious behavioral effects resulting from virtual reality experiences, and that the extent of this behavioral influence might not be known.

3. Researchers and media outlets should avoid over-hyping the benefits of virtual reality, especially when virtual reality is being discussed as a medical treatment.

4. Awareness of the problem of dual use, or using a technology for something other than its original intention, in the context of virtual reality. The authors particularly are wary of military applications for virtual reality (which are already being put to a lot of use), whether this means its use as a novel torture device or a means of decreasing a soldier's empathy for the enemy.

5. Adopting procedures that ensure a commercial virtual reality user's privacy is maintained during research at the intersection of virtual reality and the internet. Since virtual reality has the potential to record all new kinds of user information (from eye movements and emotions to the movement of a user's entire body through space), ensuring that this data is managed in a responsible way will become paramount for virtual reality researchers and commercial entities alike.

6. Privacy is also a concern when it comes to advertising. Virtual environments provide fertile new grounds for

targeted advertising, or "neuromarketing," and previous studies have shown the various ways in which virtual reality technologies might be used to significantly influence consumer behavior (especially if the virtual reality tech is being built by a company whose business model is largely based unbelievably precise user-targeted advertising, like, say, Facebook).

Despite harping on the latent dangers in emerging virtual reality technologies, Madary and Metzinger are far from Luddites. As they mention in their paper, they "fully support research into VR," and argue that there are ethical demands for *more* research in this area. Their main concern is that this research is conducted in an ethically responsible way "with the goal of mitigating harm to the general public."

Although Madary and Metzinger's code of ethics lacks a regulatory body to enforce its regulations, its publication marks an important first step toward ensuring that the proliferation of virtual reality technology doesn't lead us into some Matrix-esque hell.

"Increasingly, [the human mind] is not only culturally and socially embedded but also shaped by a technological niche that over time itself quickly acquires a rapid, autonomous dynamics and ever new properties," write Madary and Metzinger. "This creates a complex convolution… in which the biological mind and its technological niche influence each other in ways we are just beginning to understand. It is this complex convolution that makes it so important to think about the Ethics of VR in a critical, evidence-based, and rational manner."

The important caveat here is that this is all assuming that virtual reality technology becomes as ubiquitous as Zuckerberg and the other VR-evangelists are promising. There's still a decent contingent of skeptics dismissing virtual reality as a bunch of BS, and their skepticism is about to be put to the test as virtual reality tech prepares for the most stringent test a capitalist society can throw at it in the coming months: the test of commercial viability.

> *"Ultimately, such immersion might make people less willing, or even less capable, of dealing with the frustrations involved in participating in real-world marriages and family units."*

Research Should Focus on Minimizing Negative Effects of VR

Mark E. Koltko-Rivera

In the following viewpoint, Mark E. Koltko-Rivera argues that virtual reality is a powerful technology with the potential for far-ranging social and psychological impact. In this excerpt, he contends that VR could have negative effects on home and family and religion and spirituality. He suggests that technology and social science professionals cooperate in researching the effects of VR on individuals and society. Koltko-Rivera is an entrepreneur, psychologist, futurist, and media producer living in New York.

Koltko-Rivera, M. E. (2005). "The Potential Societal Impact of Virtual Reality." In K. M. Stanney & M. Zyda (eds.), *Advances in Virtual Environments Technology: Musings on Design, Evaluation, and Applications.* Volume 9 in G. Salvendy (series ed.), *HCI International 2005: 11th International Conference on Human-Computer Interaction* [CD-ROM, unpaginated]. Mahwah, NJ: Erlbaum. Copyright 2016 Mark Koltko-Rivera. All Rights Reserved. Reprinted by permission.

As you read, consider the following questions:

1. What impact does Koltko-Rivera think that virtual reality applications will have on marriage and family life?
2. What questions does the author have about the impact of virtual reality on religion and spirituality?
3. What approaches does the author recommend that VR professionals take toward researching VR?

Home and Family

Most people marry and have children; the resulting family groups have been the basic units of essentially all human cultures. What will happen when a VR simulation of this experience is available? The popularity of The Sims—"the best-selling computer game ever" (Hamilton, 2004, p. 78)—suggests that people want to try out alternative simulated lives and relationships. How will the availability of virtual family life affect people's desire or intention to pursue family life in the real world?

Consider this scenario. A single person, Jane or John Smith, ends work for the day and is at home. "Home," in a real-world sense, consists of a chair or two, a bed, a closet, a refrigerator, a table that serves as both dining and work space, a food preparation area, and a personal hygiene area, all of which fits into a studio apartment. However, this home also includes a personal VR system. Through this system, Smith lives in a mansion, with marble staircases, sauna, an Olympic-sized pool, private helipad, and other accoutrements. In this mansion lives, not only Smith, but also an attractive, caring partner, who may exist as an AI construct. Perhaps there are children as well, an entire family or extended family unit. Family and friends come by and visit, perhaps based in distributed VR networks that enable Smith's real-world friends to interact in real time, or perhaps based on AI constructs. Family life, recreation, and adventure—almost every aspect of human life, short of the intake of nutrition and the elimination of waste products—can be simulated through VR. But how will this affect the individual or society?

One can imagine different possible outcomes here. One that seems plausible is that fewer people will marry and form family units. Although marriage and family life have their benefits, they also pose inevitable challenges and frustrations. VR, on the other hand, can provide a virtual simulation of a stress-free life. One's virtual partner can be programmed to be continually and unfailingly attentive, considerate, forever youthful, and eternally compliant with the wishes of the user of the VR system. One's virtual children can be programmed to be consistently polite and deferent; some other virtual character will change the diapers. In the short run, the opportunity to visit such a virtual world might be an enticing prospect for many people. However, in the long run, continual exposure to such a virtual world might raise unrealistic expectations concerning people in the real world. Frequent immersion in such a virtual world might allow one to escape from the tasks of adult life rather than attend to them. Ultimately, such immersion might make people less willing, or even less capable, of dealing with the frustrations involved in participating in real-world marriages and family units. (Consider my earlier comments on instant gratification, of which the flip side is intolerance for frustration.)

A decrease in the rate at which marriages and family units are formed and maintained should be considered a major negative consequence. As it is, the current rates of birth in developed countries are so low as to instigate major negative consequences in society in coming years (Kotlikoff & Burns, 2004; Longman, 2004; e.g., Faiola, 2005). A development that would retard the formation of stable family units in which children would enter the world would exacerbate what already will be a difficult situation. (An exception to this might involve areas where longstanding sexist, infanticidal practices involving the selective murder of female infants has left a surplus male population; because a male surplus is associated with increased crime and even warfare [Hudson &

den Boer, 2004], it may be advisable to encourage virtual families in such areas.)

Of course, it may be argued that the availability of an escape from reality, judiciously applied, would "let off steam" and allow the person to deal with the frustrations of the real world more effectively (cf. C. Pearce, quoted in Heins & Bertin, 2002). It is difficult to see how this perspective would apply to this issue; it seems counterintuitive to think that avoidance of the family might solve family problems. However, this difference in perspectives underlines the importance of settling this question with empirical research, rather than a priori arguments.

Religion and Spirituality

We come finally to the realm of religion and spirituality. Casual investigation of the Internet suggests that many people like to involve themselves with their faith communities in a virtual way. There is even a Roman Catholic pseudo-"diocese" that exists only in virtual space (Gaillot, n.d.).

However, as can be seen with other comparisons between the Internet and virtual environments, VR has the potential to take things in a very different direction than the Internet. It is one thing to interact with others in a virtual space, and engage in the act of worshipping a god or goddess. It is another thing altogether to react in this virtual space with the gods themselves—something that VR can emulate. To go farther, it is yet another thing for one to become the embodiment of a god or goddess (the original meaning of "avatar")—another experience that VR can emulate. What might be the societal consequences of such circumstances?

One framework used in the academic psychology of religion frames religion and spirituality as having five dimensions: knowledge, ideology, ritual, emotion, and behavior (adapted from Glock, 1962). VR has the potential to heavily influence at least two of these. In terms of knowledge, all the educational potential of VR is apparent here; for example, VR makes it possible to achieve total immersion in the holy languages of one's tradition, whether that language be Sanskrit, Latin, or Sindarin. In terms of ritual, VR would give one the opportunity to conduct almost any ritual, regardless of time, place, or one's hierarchical status (e.g., not being officially consecrated as clergy).

What will it mean when spiritual rituals can be enacted virtually by anyone? At any time, or place? Will something be lost by divorcing rituals from their traditional context in time or space? Or, will the potentially greater amount of participation add to the spiritual lives of the people who enact these rituals? Will the process of being involved with an in-person worship community become passé? Or, will the experience of private spirituality change independently of the evolution of communal spirituality?

One aspect of spirituality that may be transformed thoroughly is the matter of spiritual experimentation. Such experimentation in the real world sometimes carries social consequences that are uncomfortable (e.g., being around strangers) or downright aversive (e.g., conflict with or even excommunication from one's "home" tradition). No such consequences exist in the virtual world. In American consumer culture, some people already practice a form of what some sociologists call "supermarket religion," picking what they want from this or that tradition. In the VR world of 2025, however, these opportunities will be considerably expanded. One may pick any tradition, of any time, existing in the real world or in the imagination, and try it on for size. For that matter, one may create one's own tradition, and populate it with ritual, symbol, and virtual co-worshippers (either avatars of real world humans, or AI constructs).

No doubt this will come with social consequences, as well. Will real world spiritual communities decline as virtual private spiritual pseudo-communities flourish? Or, will people try on the virtual experience and find that they now want to engage the real world counterpart? Will people reconfigure worship communities in a distributed VR environment? Will people more easily change (i.e., convert) from the religious communities of their heritage? If so, what will that do to traditions that have added some stability to their communities for millennia?

[...]

Conclusion

What would be the outcome of such research? Certainly the discovery of potential negative effects of VR technology, if any, would be sufficient motivation for engineers, social scientists, and perhaps legislative experts to consider and implement countermeasures. These might involve any number of options, from the VR equivalent of the television "V" chip to guidelines for user licenses for this technology, not to mention many software solutions. The point of this would be to minimize negative effects and maximize benefits from VR technology. VR has the potential for massive psychosocial impact. It would be wise to take a proactive approach to the matter of VR's psychosocial impact. One way to do this is for professionals both in VR engineering and in social science to cooperate in conducting research into the possible effects of this powerful, transformative technology.

> *"We can imagine powerful, inspiring*
> *religious services in virtual cathedrals*
> *... gathering huge numbers of people*
> *from all over the planet."*

Church-goers Can Find Meaning and Community in Virtual Reality

Giulio Prisco

In the following viewpoint, Giulio Prisco argues that virtual reality will be an asset to church-going people. Building on the experiences of establishing churches in Second Life, he contends that religious communities can use virtual reality to find spiritual meaning. Giulio Prisco is a virtual reality consultant and writer.

As you read, consider the following questions:

1. According to Prisco, how have churches experimented with virtual reality in the past?
2. What are some advantages that the author finds in using VR applications in a church community?
3. What are some ways that both established and yet-to-be-established religious communities can use virtual reality applications?

"Virtual Reality a New Frontier for Religions," Giulio Prisco, February 9, 2015. Reprinted by permission.

V irtual reality technology is going to radically change what it means to attend church in the next fifty years—and maybe much sooner.

While the technology is still in its infancy, however, virtual churches are limited experiments rather than significant outreach efforts—but this will change.

"Numerous persons and groups have developed churches in the virtual world, mainly Second Life," Rev. Christopher Benek told *Hypergrid Business*. "I would venture to say that most have been less concerned with true evangelical success and more focused on what their technological exploratory experience may yield in the future."

Rev. Benek serves at the largest church in the Presbytery of Tropical Florida, the First Prebyterian Church of Ft. Lauderdale, as the Associate Pastor of Family Ministries and Mission. He is also enrolled at Durham University in England where he is working on a Ph.D. in theology focusing on the intersection of technological futurism and eschatology.

For most traditional churches, virtual reality isn't even on the horizon, he said.

"But for those of us who tend to be more inclined to the developments of human technology, we are keeping abreast of the important advancements that are occurring in the virtual world," he said. "Personally, I think that as technology like Oculus Rift becomes more developed, immersive, and available to the general public, we may soon be able to easily develop virtual worship and Christian education experiences. This would be a great asset to the church universal, as it will enable the infirm, homebound, and potentially even the poor to participate from afar regardless of their personal mobility or lack of affordable transportation."

There are a number of other ways in which churches can benefit by removing physical obstacles to worship, he added.

"Congregants and pastors will be able to visit and pray with greater numbers of people more often," he said. "Small groups will be able to meet more frequently, even at great distances. The way that we currently do care and discipleship will radically change as will our expectations as to what it means to participate in those aspects of the church."

And it's not just physical barriers that virtual reality may help overcome, he added. Linguistic barriers will start coming down, as well.

"Virtual reality will allow church services to be seamlessly translated creating a more unified church body," he said.

Soon, it will be possible for thousands of simultaneous participants to congregate in virtual reality, with low latency and none of the lag problems that today's Second Life users are familiar with. That will enable the creation of massively popular online megachurches.

LifeChurch.tv is a large online church that has pioneered e-religion, initially with televised services broadcast from a central location to a network of secondary campuses and an online community. They established a presence in Second Life in 2007, but their foray into the metaverse hasn't been very successful because they treated their Second Life campus as just another physical campus. They were not creative enough and didn't design new experiences tailored to the new possibilities of virtual reality.

The story of LifeChurch.tv in Second Life is told in the book "Virtually Sacred—Myth and Meaning in World of Warcraft and Second Life," published in 2014 by Oxford University Press, by Robert Geraci, Professor in the Department of Religion at Manhattan College. Geraci argues that virtual worlds can play the role of sacred spaces, places of power where believers can engage in compelling forms of ritual behavior and form online religious communities.

The book reports that many groups in mainstream religions, including Christianity and Islam, established a virtual presence in Second Life, often bypassing institutional channels and creating grassroots communities instead. These virtual communities are often independent of traditional religious hierarchies, and much more open to inter-faith dialogue and alternative lifestyles.

Most of the metaverse churches described by Geraci have disappeared since the publication of the book, but new churches appear all the time. At this moment, the most active metaverse church is the First United Church of Christ.

The Church of the Latter Day Saints, aka the Mormon Church, has a long tradition of esoteric ritual, including re-enactments of creation and salvation mythology. Historically, those re-enactments were performed live by actors. Presently, the re-enactments are generally presented as video recordings in temples to facilitate consistency across broad distribution. Recently, the LDS has developed several new versions of the video recordings, which emphasize and nuance the mythology re-enactments in various ways, renewing many members' interest.

"I think the Church, as well as other religious organizations, would benefit from proceeding further in this direction of virtualizing and even open-sourcing their rituals," Lincoln Cannon, President of the Mormon Transhumanist Association, told *Hypergrid Business*. "Imagine authenticating to an neurally immersive online temple in which you participate in the mythological re-enactment, adapting the imagery to your personal spiritual needs, perhaps in concert with or according to the guidance of spiritual friends or authorities. I don't have a particular platform to recommend, but I do feel a great deal of inspiration from this vision of customizing and revitalizing ritual to such extent that re-enactment transcends itself and actually becomes reification: the expression of salvation mythology itself becomes transfiguration to godhood, and the expression of creation mythology itself instantiates new worlds."

The chapter "Sacred Second Lives" of *Virtually Sacred* is dedicated to new, emerging religious movements in Second Life. Perhaps more than established religions, new "native" metaverse religions will be able to take full advantage of the endless possibilities of virtual reality and offer a spiritual home to multitudes of people worldwide, especially those who search spiritual meaning independently, outside the legacy framework of mainstream religions.

ATTENDING CHURCH IN VIRTUAL REALITY

VR is, in the not too distant future, going to offer a fully immersive environment where people spend most of their time each day. This is because VR will have all of the features of our current reality plus many more [...]

For the church universal this will certainly mean drastic changes in the way that we do things. With VR, many churches won't need physical space and many will opt into beginning virtual worship experiences. The church in VR will literally become a church without walls. You won't need to drive anywhere. Just plug the family in, download your Sunday outfit, and materialize in worship.

Yes, just like now, church programs (in this case advanced software programs) will occur as well. You'll fly (yes, you can fly in VR) over to your prayer circle. Your kids will take unimaginable trips with their youth group. Everyone in the choir and praise band will sing in perfect pitch. The artistic imagery in your gathering space will change whimsically and will be fantastic. Pair all of this with advancing artificial intelligence and you just may hear the best sermon you've ever heard from your cyborg pastor.

"Virtual Reality Is Going to Change How We Experience Church," Christopher Benek, April 23, 2014. http://www.christopherbenek .com/?p=4341. Licensed under CC BY-SA 3.0.

One of Geraci's central points is that shared virtual spaces provide a sense of place, direction, and orientation, which has profound implications for religious practice. Contrary to flat web pages, in virtual reality we can build holy places, cathedrals, and sacred objects, which act as a "physical" scaffolding to hold virtual religious communities together. While vision and hearing are powerfully engaged in today's consumer 3D virtual realities, the possibility to touch objects in virtual spaces "in which the brain regions associated with grasping can potentially respond as though to conventional reality," isn't available yet to most consumers, but that will change with new interface devices.

"I'm deeply curious about how an innovative church might make use of augmented reality in its services or festivals," Geraci told *Hypergrid Business*. "It seems to me that there could be beautiful and artistic uses of something akin to the new Microsoft HoloLens. That kind of technology would actually allow people the benefits of physical community and virtual creativity. Like online churches, it could even be used to provide people with online connectivity to distant communities. Most likely, an initial introduction of such technologies would have a lot of awful, kitschy stuff happening; but there might be some real beauty and novel forms of storytelling included. In terms of a virtual-only church, I'd be curious as to what could be accomplished using something like the Oculus Rift. I have not, myself, used the rift, though; so I don't know what limitations the platform might have."

We can imagine powerful, inspiring religious services in virtual cathedrals, or in new places of worship—how about a virtual Stonehenge on the Moon—gathering huge numbers of people from all over the planet. The new virtual believers will listen to old and new words of wisdom, make friends, exchange mutual spiritual reinforcements, and contribute to their virtual communities.

Of course everything—even religion—runs on money, and how to finance virtual churches will need to be addressed. Many religious communities are self-sustaining through donations, and that financing model will still be viable. Virtual worlds have built-in payment methods, from the Linden dollar to the Bitcoin-like crypto-currency planned for High Fidelity, so that collecting donations in virtual reality will be even easier than in physical churches.

Besides recovery of survival expenses, it's well known that religion can be a profitable business as well. Other forms of financing include membership fees, merchandising, pay-only events and virtual adventures, donations from wealthy patrons, and discreet sponsorship—or even blatant in-service advertising if the virtual parishioners are willing to put up with that.

> *"Regulations and restrictions have to govern the creation and publishing of VR content, in order to protect the end-users from the possible long-term trauma."*

Virtual Reality May Not Be Safe

Vikram Kinkar

In the following viewpoint, Vikram Kinkar argues that virtual reality might have long-term psychological effects on users. He acknowledges the positive uses in which VR has proven itself, such as in training simulations, virtual travel, and entertainment. However, he warns that the immersive nature of VR might cause many to overuse the technology. Those who are drawn to adult or violent themes might be more at risk. Kinkar is a tech media expert, journalist, and editor.

As you read, consider the following questions:

1. What are some of the VR applications that Lorie Therese rates in her viewpoint as "the good"?
2. What does the author fear, in terms of titles that may be available for VR consumption?
3. What is your opinion of the author's final thought that "the benefits outweigh the risks" in virtual reality applications?

"The Dangers of Virtual Reality: It's Cool, But Is It Safe?" Vikram Kinkar, TechNorms. Reprinted by permission.

I t's like a couple of steps away where you would think you're absolutely in this world."

This is one of the reactions to virtual reality technology, as described by one of the participants of Fine Brothers Entertainment's "Elders React to Oculus Rift" video.

In the video, the participants were allowed to experience virtual reality situations, from mere mundane house tours, to roller coaster rides, and down to a scene with "Chucky," the possessed doll from the 90's, sitting with them in the room. And as another "Elder" said, the technology has the potential for being the next "Twitter," a platform that grips and causes a form of addiction and obsession for people the world over.

In yet another virtual reality experience documentary, this time, created by Complex, a participant weighed in, "There [are] going to be people who will never take that [expletive] off." In that same documentary, in which pornographic VR content was used, the same, insightful participant also mused, "[expletive] already losing their jobs for regular porn." Another participant, a female, pointed out, "I'm really afraid that [Virtual Reality] might limit the need for human interaction altogether."

Virtual Reality, via Oculus Rift, Samsung Gear VR, Google Cardboard, and other similar technologies, is fast coming into the mainstream space. So much so, that this week's major tech and mental health concern were the psychological effects of Virtual Reality.

In news that broke out into Google's trending feeds, German philosophy researchers Dr. Michael Madary and Dr. Thomas Metzinger from the Johannes Gutenberg University Mainz were quoted as being concerned about regulating the emerging medium.

Watching people react to virtual reality content in this playlist, a third-party observer would see where the concern was coming from. To quote one of the Elders reluctantly subjected to the roller coaster ride, "It actually gives you the sensation of motion." Indeed, with emerging technologies that include Cyberith's Virtualizer, a VR attachment that lets the user control the virtual reality avatar's movements with a motion pad and other components, that "sensation of motion" will get even more tactile.

The Good

On the bright side, with the Cyberith Virtualizer, exercise could be turned into a richer, more immersive experience. More than that, learning technologies such as simulations for surgery, as well as practice arenas for space travel, are being developed.

These aspects of Virtual Reality have the potential for a whole lot of good. Imagine the world where surgeons no longer need to practice on real, actual patients. There would be less mistakes from rookie surgeons who have a lot of room to grow. There may be less casualties, fatalities, from the process of learning surgery.

Imagine the world where astronauts are given very realistic space training. With these simulations, space exploration could reach new heights.

On the consumer side, VR content with the goal to allow the end-user to explore other countries, or even a world where dinosaurs coexist with modern-day people have been developed.

As several people who have experienced virtual reality devices have pointed out, this has use for the elderly or the bedridden, who are marooned at home. Or, for those who want to try extreme experiences such as skydiving or even riding a roller coaster, but do not want the risks associated with the real experience, VR could be an alternative.

The Bad

Then, there's the world where a whole slew of violent, horrific, fear-inducing, perverse content is being created and proliferated. According to this list of games with Oculus Rift support, a good majority of those titles are either violent or horror-themed games. And if a reader takes a cursory glance at the titles, pornographic and "adult" communities for Virtual Reality already exist.

While the consumption of violent, frightening, and sexually explicit content really depends on the end user's moral code, the main concern includes how the consumption of these genres of content could affect them, and the people around them.

Psychological and Social Implications

The concerns voiced by doctors of Philosophy Michael Madary and Thomas Metzinger are very real. According to reports, their team believes that the immersive technology of virtual reality may have long-term effects on those who consume VR content.

The team believes that regulations and restrictions have to govern the creation and publishing of VR content, in order to protect the end-users from the possible long-term trauma and changes that they may expose themselves to.

Even the lay people who have experienced VR were quick to point out how real the virtual reality experience is. Some who were astute also pointed out the social implications, as mentioned earlier. And with the authoritative perspective of the German researchers, indeed, this could be a concern about virtual reality technology in the long run.

Going Mainstream

An end-user could hope that the companies who plan to jump in on the emerging technologies of virtual reality would be ethical enough to ensure that their marketing strategies would have certain boundaries, and respect the effects of virtual reality on an end user's psyche. More than that, may there, indeed, be media guidelines and regulatory boundaries to govern virtual reality. Indeed, the trauma of violent and horrifying content could be long-term.

Pornographic content outside of virtual reality has already been found to have damaging effects on the brain. With immersive technology as VR, one could only imagine how much more damaging that could prove.

However, what the news on the German researchers' perspectives didn't point out is the resilience of the human mind. If Holocaust survivors could live past their extreme trauma and carve out productive lives, mere entertainment or immersive technology such as VR could be stimuli that an end user could recover from a lot quickly.

A good majority of people can take violent, horrific content without turning into serial killers and mass murderers. But is society ready to take on the minor percentage of the people who receive the stimuli and turn into violent, dangerous criminals? Or the percentage of people who won't be able to cope with the stimuli and experience effects akin to PTSD, post-traumatic stress disorder?

Well, if we look at the happy people who experienced positive virtual reality content, the benefits may outweigh the risks.

> "*These tools can bring the natural world to people. Virtual reality has the potential to bring usually inaccessible areas to people who have the power to make decisions and achieve positive change.*"

Virtual Reality Can Save the Planet

Ivy Shih

In the following viewpoint, Ivy Shih describes the potential effects of virtual reality on conservation efforts. Researchers can study endangered species and habitats without traveling to them in person. The author also believes that such access will bring greater awareness and empathy to the cause. Ivy Shih is an editor at The Conversation.

As you read, consider the following questions:

1. What has been the first application of virtual reality on conservation efforts?
2. What tools did the researchers use to create their virtual world?
3. What major benefit does the author cite regarding this virtual technology application?

V irtual reality technology is introducing a new dimension to wildlife conservation by helping researchers anywhere in the world assess the conditions of distant species and environments as if they were on location.

The first application has been to better understand the environment of endangered jaguars living in the Peruvian Amazon.

This information is being used to improve mathematical and statistical models that predict abundance and location of jaguars, as well as population trends and threats.

The approach also has applications in other regions of the world, such as protecting threatened regions of the Great Barrier Reef.

The Eyes of Researchers

The jaguar (*Panthera onca*) is currently classified as near threatened. But a lack of information on jaguar populations poses a barrier to conservation efforts.

So researchers from the Queensland University of Technology and the Lupunaluz Foundation recreated areas of the Amazon after painstakingly stitching together 360-degree video footage.

The footage will enable researchers and policy makers anywhere in the world to don a VR headset and experience the location as if they were there.

The study is unique by bringing together new virtual reality technology, local and international knowledge, and mathematical and statistical expertise, to form a strong predictive model of jaguar populations, behaviour and movement.

Professor Kerrie Mengersen, from the Queensland University of Technology, who led the expedition, said virtual reality enabled experts to enter an immersive environment so they could identify characteristics of areas where jaguars are likely to live.

"Because we can't take these experts to these inaccessible places, how could we take these places to them?" she said.

The team filmed 360-degree video using multiple cameras, including six GoPro Hero 4 camreas, and sound recording devices.

The technological set up was crucial to reconstruct the Amazon with the greatest degree of fidelity possible.

"We had a series of 360 degree camera systems, like hacked versions of GoPro used to capture video," said Associate Professor Tomasz Bednarz, also from the Queensland University of Technology, who was instrumental in the set up of the project.

"We also had recording systems to capture the sounds of the environment from all directions."

Mengersen told The Conversation that this method preserved more detailed information compared with computer generated virtual reality environments developed in a pilot study with rock wallabies in Australia.

"The experts needed to know about the type of rocks to make any judgements about habitat suitability for the wallabies, and it is that degree of small scale detail that was really hard to obtain in our computer generated environments," Mengersen said.

"But immersive environments using 360-degree photos and video can give us that."

The virtual reality footage from the Amazon enabled experts to identify tree species that jaguar would frequent or fruiting species that would attract their prey.

The information will be used by the Lupunaluz Foundation and the big cat charity Pantherato to guide policy decisions and to help establish "jaguar corridors." These are safe roads of passage between fragmented sections of the jaguar's habitat.

Bringing the Natural World to the People

Dr Megan Saunders, a marine ecologist in the Global Change Institute at the University of Queensland, said virtual reality technology could help engage the public with conservation issues.

"It has the potential to explain to people the importance of preserving the environment," she said.

One similar project is the XL Catlin Seaview Survey, which uses 360-degree imaging to monitor coral reefs around the world

WITHDRAWING INTO VIRTUAL REALITY

An unprecedented phenomenon is quickly taking over Japan. "Hikikomori," literally meaning "to pull inward," has young people, who would normally enter the workforce and create families, opting out for staying at their parents' houses and immersing themselves in digital entertainment instead.

The results of such new lifestyle are harrowing: birth rates in Japan are rapidly declining, and the country has seen a plunging downward trend in employment rates. But this dangerous combination of economic ennui and social isolation is not just a Japanese problem.

The youth of the Western world is starting to shrivel as well.

With the market of virtual reality booming as ever, we are forced to answer the inevitable, yet highly dreaded question: despite all the positive adaptations, what are the true implications of VR technology on our mundane existence?

Will it encourage the trend of social withdrawal by giving more dejected adolescents access to easy rewards without effort? Is it ill-advised to take someone with a tentative grasp on social interaction and give them an all-immersive multimedia experience, which is yet another reason to stay home instead of making connections or seeking fulfillment? Is it going to alter our very sense of self?

"The Other Side of Virtual Reality and Its Impact on Our Everyday Lives," Chris Altman, April 2016.

in the form of high-resolution panoramic images, which are made available to the research community.

The most recent expedition was to Heron Island to survey the widespread coral bleaching on the Great Barrier Reef.

"These tools can bring the natural world to people," Dr Saunders said. "Virtual reality has the potential to bring usually inaccessible areas to people who have the power to make decisions and achieve positive change."

Periodical and Internet Sources Bibliography

The following articles have been selected to supplement the diverse views presented in this chapter.

Murad Ahmed, "What's the Future of Virtual Reality?" World Economic Forum, January 5, 2016.

Sheryar Ali, Samuel Vaughn, and James Williams, "Physiological and Psychological Effects of Virtual Reality," *Medium,* April 9, 2015.

Scott Gerber, "Virtual Reality Will Change Business as We Know It," *Readwrite*, March 9, 2016.

Larry Greenemeier, "Virtual Reality for All, Finally," *Scientific American*, December 8, 2015.

Michael Madary, "Are Virtual Reality Experiences Safe from an Ethical Point of View?," European Commission, March 9, 2016.

Doug Magyari, "Virtual Reality: Are Health Risks Being Ignored?" CNBC, January 8, 2016.

Brian Shuster, "Could Virtual Reality Revitalize the Economy?," *Wired*, 2014.

Tracey Taylor, "Will Virtual Reality Be the New Normal?" *The Pulse*, December 20, 2014.

Artin Terhakopian, "Embracing Virtual Reality," *TIME,* April 3, 2013.

Teensafe, "The Virtual World Is Real. Here's How It'll Affect Your Teen," May 5, 2016.

Fred Turner, "The Politics of Virtual Reality," *American Prospect*, July 12, 2015.

For Further Discussion

Chapter 1

1. Despite promising research, what are the major limitations to using VR applications in education?
2. In what areas of health care has virtual reality shown the most potential for positive outcomes?
3. Although the American military has embraced virtual reality for training, what might be some drawbacks to using this technology?

Chapter 2

1. Using at least two viewpoints as evidence, what might be serious challenges to VR becoming mainstream technology?
2. How might virtual reality technology be successfully implemented in the business world?
3. Explain how researchers are using virtual reality to investigate people's emotional lives?

Chapter 3

1. How has VR technology has been used to treat patients suffering from phobias?
2. Using at least two viewpoints as evidence, explain the impact of immersion and presence on the success of VR used in psychological research.
3. What are the dangers in using VR technology to play violent games?

Chapter 4

1. Several authors warn about the dangers of VR overuse. What are some of their concerns?

2. Explain how those interested in a spiritual community might use VR technology?

3. In your opinion, what are some regulations and restrictions, if any, VR developers should adopt when creating content?

Organizations to Contact

The editors have compiled the following list of organizations concerned with the issues debated in this book. The descriptions are derived from materials provided by the organizations. All have publications or information available for interested readers. The list was compiled on the date of publication of the present volume; the information provided here may change. Be aware that many organizations take several weeks or longer to respond to inquiries, so allow as much time as possible.

Family Research Center Virtual Reality Laboratory
Department of Psychology, Southern Methodist University, PO Box 750442, Dallas, TX 75275-0442
Phone: (214) 768-4994
Website: www.smu.edu/Dedman/Academics/Departments/Psychology/Research/FamilyResearchCenter/Research/Virtual-Reality

The Family Research Center's virtual reality laboratory supports simulation software designed for the study and prevention of violence. A fully interactive experience, the virtual reality technology creates realistic, ecologically valid situations for observing teens' behavior in social interactions that present the opportunity to intervene as a bystander.

Human Interface Technology Laboratory
University of Washington, Box 352142, Seattle, WA 98195-2142
Email: tfurness@u.washington.edu
Website: www.hitl.washington.edu

The Human Interface Technology Lab (HITLab) is a multi-disciplinary research and development lab whose work centers around human interface technology. Lab researchers represent a wide range of departments from across the University of

Washington campus, including engineering, medicine, education, social sciences, architecture and the design arts.

Institute for Creative Technologies
12015 Waterfront Drive, Playa Vista, CA 900094-2536
Phone: (310) 574-5700
Email: info@ict.usc.edu
Website: ict.usc.edu

Established in 1999 and sponsored by the U.S. Army, ICT brings film and game industry artists together with computer and social scientists to develop immersive environments for military training, health therapies, science education, and more.

Rehabilitation Games &
Virtual Reality (ReGame VR) Laboratory
Northeastern University, 360 Huntington Ave, Boston, MA 02115
Phone: (616) 373-2000
Email: regamevrlab@neu.edu
Website: www.northeastern.edu/regamevrlab

The ReGameVR lab focuses on promoting the sustainable, evidence-based integration of virtual reality (VR) and active video gaming systems into rehabilitation. Researchers explore how VR-based therapy can improve motor learning, balance, functional mobility, and participation in children and adults with neuromotor impairments.

The Virtual Environment and Multimodal Interaction (VEMI) Laboratory
VEMI Lab, University of Maine, Carnegie Hall, Orono, ME 04469
Phone: (207) 581-2151
Website: https://umaine.edu/vemi

The VEMI Lab is an educational, research, and development facility based on a collaborative model where faculty, undergraduate, and graduate students across more than a dozen disciplines learn about scientific research, creative design, and technical skills using the latest virtual and augmented reality technologies.

Virtual Human Interaction Lab

McClatchy Hall, Room 411, Department of Communication, Stanford University, Stanford, CA 94305-2050
Phone: (650) 736-8848
Email: vhil@stanfordvr.com
Website: vhil.stanford.edu

The mission of the Virtual Human Interaction Lab is to understand the dynamics and implications of interactions among people in immersive virtual reality simulations (VR) and other forms of human digital representations in media, communication systems, and games. Their work is centered on using empirical, behavioral science methodologies to explore people as they interact in these digital worlds.

Virtual Reality Applications Center

Iowa State University, 1620 Howe Hall, 537 Bissell Road, Ames, IA, 50011-2274
Phone (515) 294-3092
Email: vrac@iastate.edu
Website: www.vrac.iastate.edu

Iowa State University's Virtual Reality Applications Center (VRAC) is an interdisciplinary research center focused at the intersection of humans and technology, aimed broadly at enhancing the productivity and creativity of people. The VRAC's world-class research infrastructure supports the research of faculty and students representing all seven of ISU's colleges, as well as the interests of collaborators from several federal agencies and numerous industry partners.

Virtual Reality Research Group

Institute of Psychiatry, Psychology & Neuroscience, King's College London, Strand, London Wc2RsLS, United Kingdom
Phone: +44 (0) 20 7836 5454
Email: lucia.valmaggia@kcl.ac.uk
Website: www.kcl.ac.uk/ioppn/depts/psychology/research/ResearchGroupings/VRRG/Virtual-Reality-Research-Group.aspx

The Virtual Reality (VR) Lab is a multidisciplinary group of clinical academics, neuroscientists, post-docs, and students. Their work aims to improve the understanding of the mechanisms that play a role in the onset and maintenance of mental health problems. They develop new assessment and treatment VR environments to improve the well-being in people with mental health problems.

Virtual World Society

PO Box 15539, Seattle WA, 98105
Website: virtualworldsociety.org

The Virtual World Society (VWS) is a global network of pioneers, developers, resources, events, and organizations that are committed to advancing the power of virtual worlds for the good of society. Its website provides a variety of resources for readers interested in learning more about virtual reality.

The VR/AR Association

20 S. Sarah Street, St. Louis, MO 63108
Website: www.thevrara.com

The VR/AR Association (The VRARA) is an international organization designed to foster collaboration between innovative companies and people in the virtual reality and augmented reality ecosystem that accelerates growth, fosters research and education, helps develop industry standards, connects member organizations, and promotes the services of member companies.

Bibliography of Books

Steve Aukstakalnis, *Practical Augmented Reality: A Guide to the Technologies, Applications, and Human Factors for AR and VR.* Indianapolis, IN: Addison Wesley, 2016.

Dong Hwa Choi, Amber Dailey-Hebert, and Judi Simmons Estes, *Emerging Tools and Applications of Virtual Reality in Education.* Hershey, PA: Information Science Reference, 2016.

Andrea Diem-Lane, *The Avatar Project: Virtual Reality, AI, and the Future of Education.* Walnut, CA: Mt. San Antonio College, 2016.

Jason Jerald, *The VR Book: Human-Centered Design for Virtual Reality.* San Rafael, CA: Morgan & Claypool Publishers, 2016.

Kevin Kelly, *The Inevitable: Understanding the 12 Technological Forces That Will Shape Our Future.* New York, NY: Viking, 2016.

Minhua Ma, Lakhmi C. Jain, and Paul Anderson, eds., *Virtual, Augmented Reality and Serious Games for Healthcare 1.* New York, NY: Springer, 2014.

Robert M. McLay, *Battling Post Traumatic Stress Disorder with Virtual Reality.* Baltimore, MD: Johns Hopkins University Press, 2012.

Tony Parisi, *Learning Virtual Reality: Developing Immersive Experiences and Applications for Desktop, Web, and Mobile.* Sebastopol, CA: O'Reilly Media, 2016.

Robert Riener and Matthias Harders, *Virtual Reality in Medicine.* New York: Springer, 2016.

Alec Ross, *The Industries of the Future.* New York, NY: Simon & Schuster, 2016.

Michael Saler, *As If: Modern Enchantment and the Literary Prehistory of Virtual Reality.* Oxford, UK: Oxford University Press, 2012.

Patrice L. Tamar Weiss, Emily A. Keshner, and Mindy F. Levin, eds., *Virtual Reality for Physical and Motor Rehabilitation.* New York, NY: Springer, 2014.

Clint Zeagler, Thad Starner, Tavenner Hall, and Maria Wong Sala, *Meeting the Challenge: The Path Towards A Consumer Wearable Computer.* Atlanta, GA: Georgia Institute of Technology, 2015.

Index